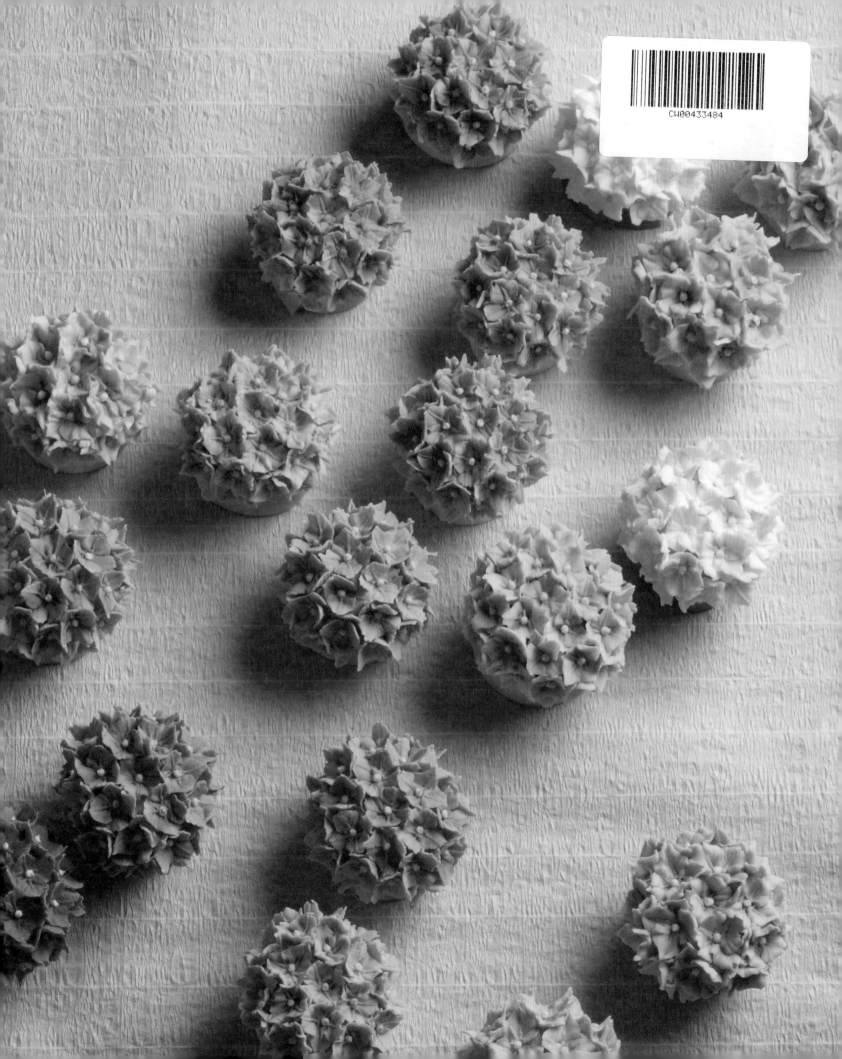

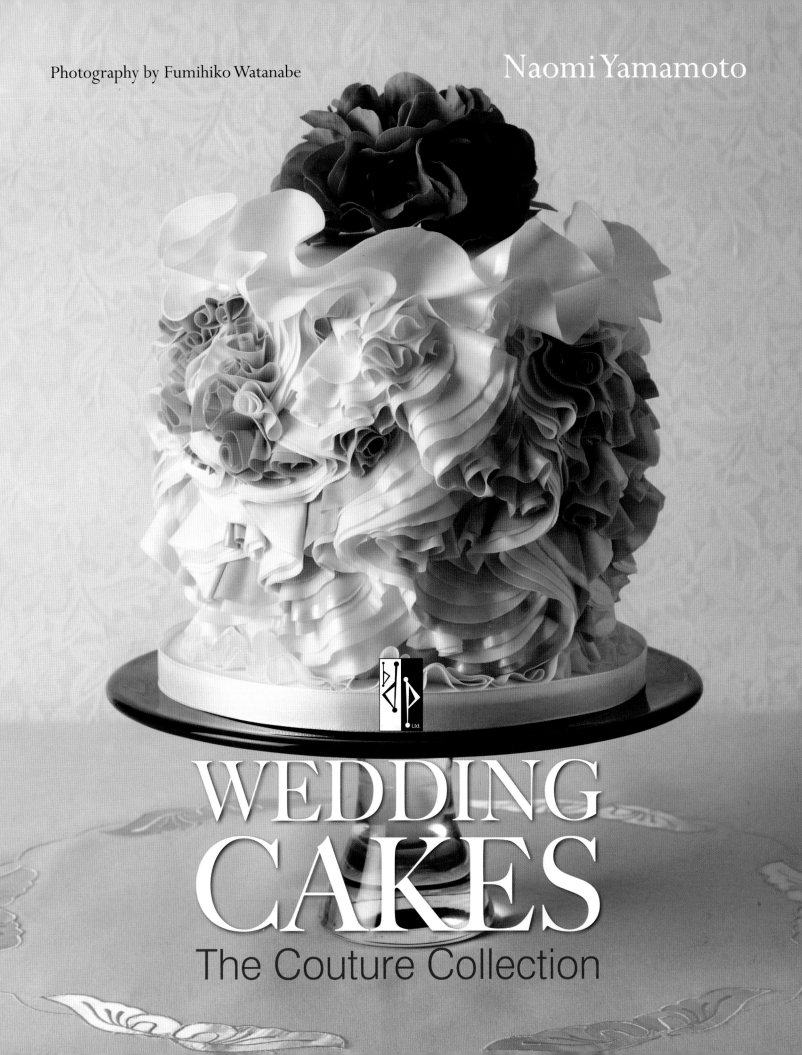

Photography by Fumihiko Watanabe

Naomi Yamamoto

WEDDING CAKES

The Couture Collection

Dedication

To my wonderful family – my husband Seiji, my daughter Seiko and her lovely family Nicolas and Didier – with all my love and gratitude.

Acknowledgements

It was challenging for the team at Squires Kitchen and me to collaborate on this book because of the great distance between the UK and Japan. I appreciate everyone's patience and devotion both in Farnham and Tokyo, despite this inconvenience. Special thanks goes to Beverley and Robert Dutton for giving me this exciting opportunity, and to Jenny, Frankie and Sarah for putting this beautiful book together.

I would like to express my gratitude to two special people, Ayako and Sachiko. Ayako is a flower designer and runs A's Flower in London and also teaches flower arranging at Squires Kitchen International School. Her artistic flair and dependability helped me work together with Squires Kitchen easily and successfully. Sachiko, a professional editor in Japan and also a passionate sugarcrafter, gave me precious technical advice throughout. Without their help, my book would not have been possible.

I would also like to say a big thank you to Etsuko of Etsuko Sugimoto Bakery School, for being my most reliable adviser on baking.

And last but not least, I would like to thank my family. They are, and always will be, my greatest supporters.

First published in March 2013 by B. Dutton Publishing Limited, The Grange, Hones Business Park, Farnham, Surrey, GU9 8BB.

Copyright: Naomi Yamamoto 2013

ISBN-13: 978-1-905113-40-8

Publisher: Beverley Dutton

Group Editor: Jenny Stewart

Art Director/Designer: Sarah Ryan

Editor: Jenny Royle

Designer: Zena Deakin

Graphic Designers: Louise Pepé and Abbie Johnston

Copy Editor: Amy Norman

Editorial Assistants: Frankie New and Adele Duthie

PR and Advertising Manager: Natalie Bull

Photography: Fumihiko Watanabe

Translation of projects: Miyoko Ito

Interpreter: Ayako Saida

Printed in China

Important Information

The Author and Publisher have made every effort to ensure that the contents of this book will not cause harm or injury or pose any danger. Please note that some inedible items, such as floral wires and cocktail sticks, have been used in the projects in this book. All such inedible items must be removed before the cakes are eaten. Similarly, any non food-grade equipment and substances must not come into contact with any food that is to be eaten. Neither the Author nor the Publisher can be held responsible for errors or omissions and cannot accept liability for injury, damage or loss to persons or property, however it may arise, as a result of acting upon guidelines and information printed in this book.

Introduction

When Squires Kitchen first published Wedding Cakes– A Design Source in 1999 I submitted photos of my cakes to the magazine from Japan. Beverley Dutton kindly included them in the following issues and this is how our relationship started. This beautiful book is a result of our continuous friendship with much respect and professionalism, and I, above all, would like to thank Beverley and Robert very much.

Culture and customs vary from country to country. Japan is no exception and people here celebrate a wedding very differently to those in Europe. However, in spite of this I believe that a beautifully decorated wedding cake appeals to everyone in the world, whatever their background or culture. This is my belief and has been my motivation whilst working on this book.

There is a Japanese saying describing the beauty of a woman which perfectly describes the beauty of a bride on her wedding day:

"立てば芍薬，座れば牡丹，歩く姿は百合の花"

('She is standing like a peony, sitting like a tree peony and walking as an Easter lily'). Just like this saying, I have tried to create lovely, elegant wedding cakes with popular, well-known flowers, as flower motifs always add a natural and gentle touch to a cake.

With regards to sugarcraft techniques, throughout the book I have tried to include many photos alongside detailed descriptions to show each process in as much detail as possible. I hope that the introductory chapters on sugar flowers and royal icing will also be very helpful for readers.

Making a wedding cake for someone special is certainly an honour and very gratifying, yet if you try to include too much decoration, the work can sometimes overpower the cake. For heavily decorated designs the key is to use a lightweight dummy cake to decorate; the lighter the cake, the more flexibility you will have with the decoration and you will avoid damaging the real cake. Real cakes can be used for the simpler tiers in the design or as separate cutting cakes – I have included some of my favourite recipes at the beginning of the book. Another technique I sometimes use is to create a cake board beside the wedding cake with a design that matches the main cake.

Whatever design you are making it is important to relax when you make a wedding cake and enjoy the moment!

Over the past ten years, trends in the sugarcraft world have changed – I hope that my book will stay attractive and helpful for sugarcraft lovers for many years to come.

Contents

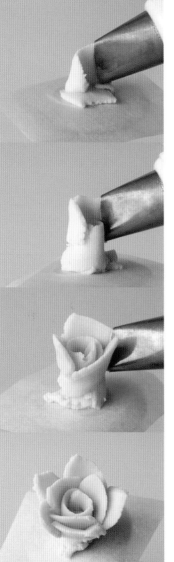

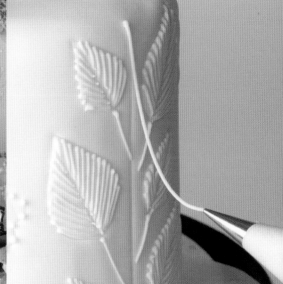

PROJECTS

Edibles and Equipment

You will need the same basic items for most of the projects in this book, so if you make cakes regularly it is worth investing in any items that you don't already have. Any specific requirements for either edibles or equipment are listed at the beginning of each cake so make sure you have everything you need before you start a project. All of the items are readily available from sugarcraft suppliers, see page 196.

Basic equipment

1	Acetate sheet	17	Pencil (HB)
2	Aluminium foil	18	Piping bags
3	Cake cards, boards and drums	19	Piping nozzles
4	Cake dowels	20	Rolling pins, large and small
5	Cake smoothers	21	Rubber spatula
6	Cake spacers	22	Ruler (50cm (20") if possible)
7	Cake and cupcake tins	23	Saucepans
8	Cling film (not pictured)	24	Satin ribbon
9	Cocktail sticks	25	Scissors
10	Dress pins	26	Serrated knife, large
11	Electric mixer	27	Sharp knife
12	Flower nail	28	Side scraper
13	Greaseproof/tracing paper	29	Sieve
14	Kitchen/tissue paper	30	Tea strainer
15	Non-stick boards, large and small	31	Turntable
16	Palette knives, large, medium and small	32	Weighing scales
		33	Wire cutters/pliers

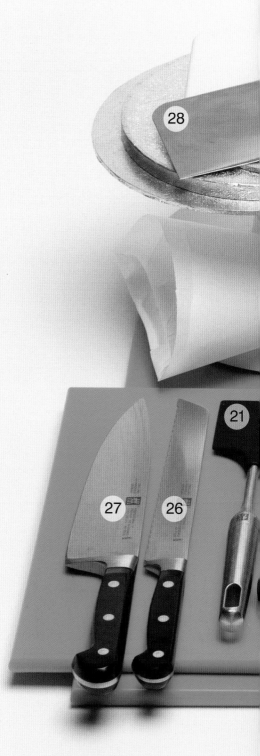

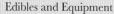

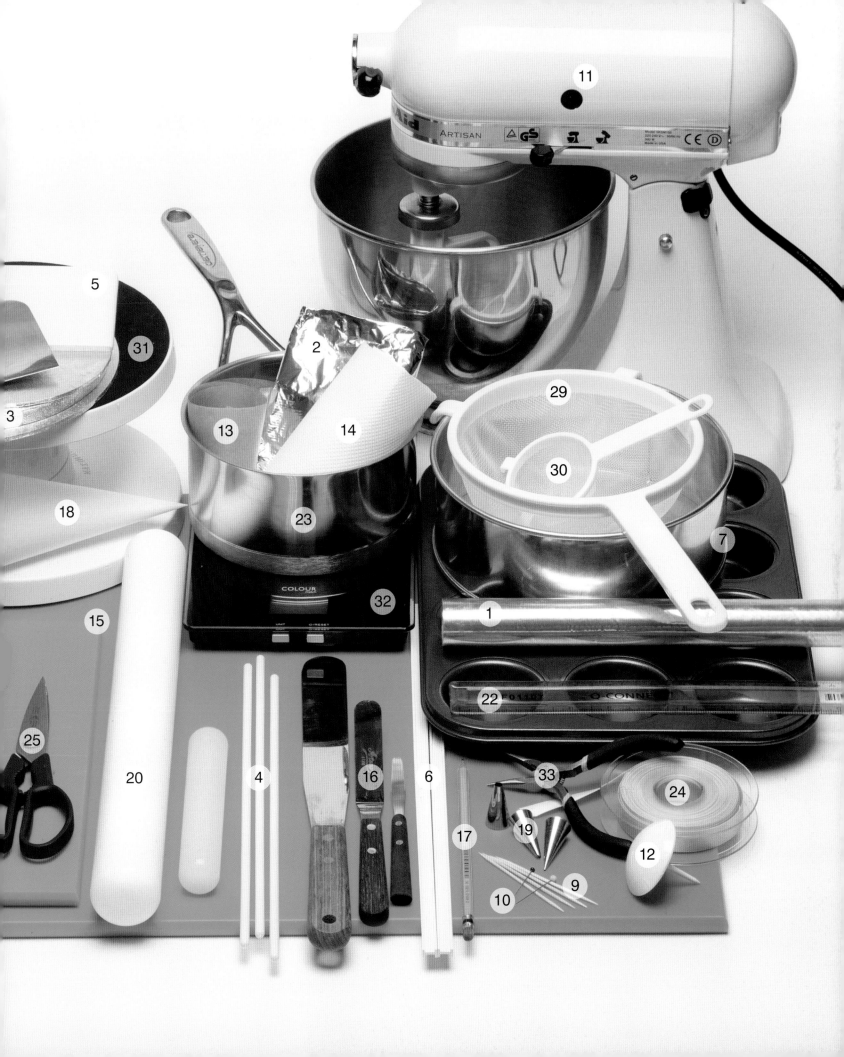

Sugarcraft/sugar flower equipment

1 Ball tool

2 Bamboo skewer or flower veiner

3 Bone tool

4 CelPin

5 Cotton thread

6 Cutting wheel (not pictured)

7 Dusting brushes

8 Fine pointed scissors

9 Floral tape: green

10 Floral wires (green and white)

11 Flower/leaf shaping tool

12 Flower stand

13 Foam pad

14 Garrett frill cutter

15 Leaf veiners, including dried corn husk (not pictured)

16 Metal petal cutters

17 Paintbrushes

18 Pasta machine (not pictured)

19 Plastic flower cutters, large

20 Polystyrene balls (2cm–6cm)

21 Posy picks

22 Quilting tool (not pictured)

23 Scribing needle (not pictured)

24 Silk veining tool (not pictured)

25 Tissue paper (not pictured)

26 Tweezers

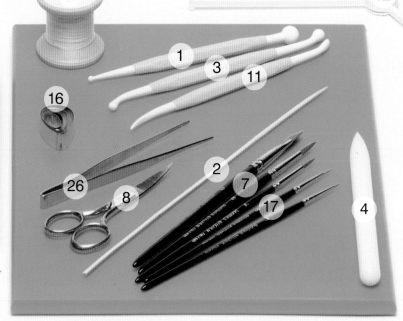

Recipes and Baking Charts

How to line a cake tin

You will need

Cake tin

Greaseproof paper or baking (parchment) paper

Pencil

Pair of scissors

White vegetable fat/shortening

1 If you are using greaseproof paper rather than baking parchment, lightly grease the inside of the tin (base and sides) with white vegetable fat.

2 Place the cake tin on top of a piece of greaseproof paper/baking parchment, draw around the base of the tin with a pencil and cut along the line with a pair of scissors.

3 For a round tin, cut a strip of paper that is as long as the circumference of the tin and slightly wider than the height of the tin. For a tin with straight sides, cut a strip to fit around the inside of the tin, again slightly wider than the height of the tin, and crease the paper at the corners.

4 Place the greaseproof paper from step 2 in the base of the tin and the longer strip of paper around the sides. Stick down the ends of the strip with vegetable fat. Make sure there are no gaps and that the paper fits neatly in the tin.

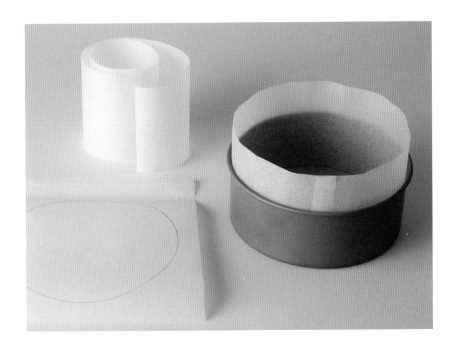

Tips for baking cakes

- The best cakes for covering are ones that are quite firm and will last a long time, such as fruit cakes or butter sponges.

- Always bake a cake on the middle shelf of the oven: the top and bottom shelves get slightly hotter and may cause your cake to burn.

- Baking times vary from oven to oven and power differs from country to country: once the cake has risen and becomes lightly golden brown the best way to gauge if your cake is done is by gently pressing the top of the cake. If the cake springs back to the touch then your cake is ready. Alternatively, insert a metal skewer into the middle of the cake for three seconds. If the skewer comes out hot and clean, the cake is baked.

- Once baked, remove the cake from the oven and leave it to cool in the tin. To cool the cake down more quickly and to prevent it from shrinking, whilst the cake is still in the tin drop it from approximately 20cm (7¾") high onto a heatproof work surface. This will help expel the hot air.

- If you are baking an unusual size or shape of cake and are unsure how much cake mix to prepare, fill the cake tin you want to use ²/₃ full with water and then weigh it. This amount will tell you how much cake mix you need to fill the tin.

Butter sponge cake quantities

Round	10cm (4")	15cm (6")	18cm (7")	20cm (8")	23cm (9")	25cm (10")	28cm (11")	30cm (12")
Square		13cm (5")	15cm (6")	18cm (7")	20cm (8")	23cm (9")	25cm (10")	28cm (11")
Butter, unsalted (softened)	50g (1¾oz)	150g (5¼oz)	200g (7oz)	250g (8¾oz)	350g (12¼oz)	450g (1lb)	550g (1lb 3½oz)	650g (1lb 7oz)
Caster sugar	50g (1¾oz)	150g (5¼oz)	200g (7oz)	250g (8¾oz)	350g (12¼oz)	450g (1lb)	550g (1lb 3½oz)	650g (1lb 7oz)
Self-raising flour (sifted)	50g (1¾oz)	150g (5¼oz)	200g (7oz)	250g (8¾oz)	350g (12¼oz)	450g (1lb)	550g (1lb 3½oz)	650g (1lb 7oz)
Eggs (approx. 50g each)	1	3	4	5	7	9	11	13
Vanilla extract	⅓tsp	1tsp	1⅓tsp	1⅔tsp	2⅓tsp	3tsp	1¼tbsp	1⅓tbsp
Baking time (approx.)	40mins	50mins	50mins	1hr	1hr 15mins	1hr 20mins	1hr 40mins	2hrs

Butter sponge cake

There are two methods you can use to bake a butter sponge cake: the all-in-one method and the sugar–butter method. There is not much difference between the two recipes, but I personally find that if I use the all-in-one method my cakes are more delicious and have a finer crumb.

All-in-one method

1 Preheat the oven to 160°C/320°F/gas mark 2–3 and line the cake tin (see page 9). If the cake is likely to rise higher than the depth of the tin (i.e. if the cake mixture fills more than ¾ of the tin), line the sides with a strip of paper that is 4cm–5cm (1¾"–2") more than the depth of the tin.

2 Place the eggs in a mixing bowl, add the vanilla extract to the eggs and mix.

3 Place the eggs and the vanilla extract with the flour, sugar and butter into the bowl of an electric mixer. Mix together with the paddle attachment on a low speed at first and then increase the speed and continue to mix until the batter is combined.

4 Pour the mixture into the tin and use a spatula to spread out the mixture evenly. Place in the centre of the oven and bake it for the required time or until a skewer inserted into the cake comes out hot and clean (see page 9).

Sugar–butter method

1 Preheat the oven to 160°C/320°F/gas mark 2–3 and line the cake tin (see page 9). If the cake is likely to rise higher than the depth of the tin (i.e. if the cake mixture fills more than ¾ of the tin), line the sides with a strip of paper that is 4cm–5cm (1¾"–2") higher than the depth of the tin.

2 Place the eggs in a mixing bowl, add the vanilla extract to the eggs and mix.

3 Place the butter and sugar together in the bowl of a mixer and beat together with the paddle attachment until light and fluffy. Add about 10% of the flour to the mixture and mix in thoroughly.

4 Gradually add the eggs with the vanilla to the mixture, beating well after each addition.

5 Mix in the remaining flour at a low speed until thoroughly combined.

6 Pour the mixture into the tin and use a spatula to spread out the mixture evenly. Place in the centre of the oven and bake it for the required time or until a skewer inserted into the cake comes out hot and clean (see page 9).

Fruit cake quantities

Round	10cm (4")	15cm (6")	18cm (7")	20cm (8")	23cm (9")	25cm (10")	28cm (11")	30cm (12")
Square		13cm (5")	15cm (6")	18cm (7")	20cm (8")	23cm (9")	25cm (10")	28cm (11")
Currants	40g (1½oz)	100g (3½oz)	130g (4½oz)	165g (5¾oz)	230g (8¼oz)	300g (10½oz)	360g (12½oz)	420g (14¾oz)
Sultanas	40g (1½oz)	100g (3½oz)	130g (4½oz)	165g (5¾oz)	230g (8¼oz)	300g (10½oz)	360g (12½oz)	420g (14¾oz)
Raisins	40g (1½oz)	100g (3½oz)	130g (4½oz)	165g (5¾oz)	230g (8¼oz)	300g (10½oz)	360g (12½oz)	420g (14¾oz)
Glacé cherries	15g (½oz)	30g (1oz)	45g (1½oz)	55g (2oz)	75g (2½oz)	100g (3½oz)	120g (4½oz)	140g (5oz)
Orange peel	15g (½oz)	30g (1oz)	45g (1½oz)	55g (2oz)	75g (2½oz)	100g (3½oz)	120g (4½oz)	140g (5oz)
Lemon peel	15g (½oz)	30g (1oz)	45g (1½oz)	55g (2oz)	75g (2½oz)	100g (3½oz)	120g (4½oz)	140g (5oz)
Lemons (zest)	¼	⅓	½	½	¾	1	1⅓	2
Brandy	50ml (1¾fl oz)	100ml (3½fl oz)	150ml (5¼fl oz)	200ml (7fl oz)	270ml (9½fl oz)	360ml (12½fl oz)	430ml (15fl oz)	500ml (17½fl oz)
Butter, unsalted (softened)	60g (2oz)	150g (5¼oz)	200g (7oz)	250g (8¾oz)	350g (12¼oz)	450g (1lb)	550g (1lb 3½oz)	650g (1lb 7oz)
Brown sugar	60g (2oz)	150g (5¼oz)	200g (7oz)	250g (8¾oz)	350g (12¼oz)	450g (1lb)	550g (1lb 3½oz)	650g (1lb 7oz)
Plain flour	60g (2oz)	150g (5¼oz)	200g (7oz)	250g (8¾oz)	350g (12¼oz)	450g (1lb)	550g (1lb 3½oz)	650g (1lb 7oz)
Eggs (approx. 50g each)	1	2⅔	3⅔	4½	6⅓	8	10	11⅔
Baking powder	¼tsp	½tsp	⅔tsp	¾tsp	1¼tsp	1½tsp	1¾tsp	2⅓tsp
Mixed spice	½tsp	¾tsp	1tsp	1¼tsp	1⅔tsp	2¼tsp	2¾tsp	3⅓tsp
Black treacle	2tsp	1⅓tbsp	1⅔tbsp	2tbsp	3tbsp	3⅔tbsp	4⅓tbsp	6tbsp
Baking time	1hr	2½hrs	3hrs	3¼hrs	3⅓hrs	3½hrs	4hrs	4½hrs

Fruit cake

Fruit cakes need a long time in the oven to ensure they are baked thoroughly: it is a good idea to put two baking trays under the cake tin when you place it in the oven, and cover the cake with tin foil once it becomes golden brown to prevent it from burning (especially with larger cakes).

1 Place the dried fruits in a bowl of boiling water and then use a sieve to drain them quickly.

2 Chop the glacé cherries into small pieces and place in a bowl with the orange and lemon peel and dried fruit. Grate in the lemon zest and add the brandy to the mixture. Mix them together well and leave to soak for at least one day. Once soaked, use a sieve to strain the fruit over a bowl.

3 Preheat the oven to 150°C/300°F/gas mark 2 and line a cake tin with a double layer of greaseproof paper or baking parchment (see page 9).

4 Place the eggs in a bowl and beat lightly.

5 In another bowl or in an electric mixer with the paddle attachment, cream the butter and sugar together until light and fluffy. Add the treacle and mix in well.

6 Add 10% of the flour to the mixture, mix in well and then gradually add the eggs, beating well after each addition.

7 Sieve the remaining flour, baking powder and spice together, add to the mixture and mix in thoroughly. Add the soaked fruits and fold them in with a spatula.

8 Pour the cake mixture into the prepared tin and smooth the top of the mixture with a spatula.

9 Bake the cake for the required time or until a skewer inserted into the cake comes out hot and clean (see page 9).

10 Once the cake is baked, take it out of the oven and leave it to cool in the tin.

11 Drizzle the remaining brandy over the top of the cake.

To store, wrap the fruit cake in greaseproof paper when cool and then double wrap in cling film. The flavour of this fruit cake will improve if you store it in the refrigerator for three days before serving. This cake will keep for 2–3 weeks.

Chocolate cake quantities

Round	10cm (4")	15cm (6")	18cm (7")	20cm (8")	23cm (9")	25cm (10")	28cm (11")	30cm (12")
Square	7.5cm (3")	12cm (5")	15cm (6")	18cm (7")	20cm (8")	23cm (9")	25cm (10")	28cm (11")
Butter, unsalted (softened)	80g (2¾oz)	195g (6¾oz)	260g (9oz)	330g (11½oz)	455g (1lb)	590g (1lb 5oz)	710g (1lb 9½oz)	900g (2lb)
Dark (semi-sweet) couverture chocolate drops (minimum 50% cocoa solids)	75g (2½oz)	180g (6¼oz)	240g (8½oz)	300g (10½oz)	420g (14¾oz)	540g (1lb 3oz)	660g (1lb 7¼oz)	840g (1lb 13oz)
Flour	60g (2oz)	150g (5¼oz)	200g (7oz)	250g (8¾oz)	350g (12¼oz)	450g (1lb)	550g (1lb 3½oz)	650g (1lb 7oz)
Caster sugar	60g (2oz)	150g (5¼oz)	200g (7oz)	250g (8¾oz)	350g (12¼oz)	450g (1lb)	550g (1lb 3½oz)	650g (1lb 7oz)
Eggs (approx. 50g each)	1	3	4	5	7	9	11	13
Baking powder	⅓tsp	1tsp	1⅓tsp	1⅔tsp	2⅓tsp	1tbsp	1⅓tbsp	1⅓tbsp
Vanilla extract	⅓tsp	1tsp	1⅓tsp	1⅔tsp	2⅓tsp	1tbsp	1⅓tbsp	1⅓tbsp
Baking time	45mins	1hr	1hr 15mins	1hr 15mins	1hr 20mins	1hr 30mins	1hr 45mins	2hrs

Chocolate cake

I always use good quality dark (semi-sweet) chocolate for this recipe as this gives the cake a wonderfully rich flavour.

1 Boil some water in a saucepan and place the chocolate drops in a metal bowl over the saucepan. Ensure that the bowl does not touch the water otherwise the chocolate will seize. Melt the chocolate then leave to cool slightly.

2 Place the eggs in a bowl, add the vanilla extract and mix together well.

3 Preheat the oven to 160°C/315°F/gas mark 2–3 and line the cake tin (see page 9).

4 Place the softened butter and sugar in the bowl of an electric mixer and use a paddle attachment to beat them together until light and fluffy. Add about 10% of the flour to the mixture and mix in well.

5 Gradually add the eggs and vanilla extract to the mixture, beating well after each addition.

6 Add the melted chocolate and mix until well combined.

7 Sieve the remaining flour and baking powder together into the mixture and mix at a low speed until well combined.

8 Pour the mixture into the tin and use a spatula to spread out the mixture evenly.

9 Bake in the oven for the required time or until a skewer inserted comes out hot and clean (see page 9).

Rum balls

This is my favourite recipe to make with any leftover trimmings of the cake and any filling. It is very easy to make and a great way of using up any leftover ingredients as you can adjust the recipe depending on the amount of leftovers. You can also use this recipe to make cake pops – just insert a lollipop stick into the bottom of the cake ball.

You will need

100g (3½oz) cake trimmings

40g (1½oz) chocolate ganache (or melted chocolate)

20g (¾oz) buttercream (or single cream)

30g (1oz) raisins soaked in rum (see page 20)

A small amount of another filling (e.g. raspberry jam, maraschino cherries) (optional)

Unsweetened cocoa powder

Makes about 7 x 3cm (1⅛) balls

1 Bring the chocolate ganache and buttercream to room temperature.

2 Place the cake trimmings in a bowl and use a fork to break them into small pieces. You could also use a food processor to do this.

3 Add all the ingredients, except the buttercream, and mix in well.

4 Add enough buttercream to hold the mixture together and mix in well.

5 Place a piece of cling film over your hand and scoop up a small handful of dough. Wrap up the cling film, twist the open end closed and squeeze the dough to make a ball.

6 Once you have made a ball, remove the dough from the cling film. If the dough is too soft, place the cake balls on a tray and leave them in the refrigerator to firm up. Place the cocoa powder in a bowl and then roll each ball of dough in the powder to coat it.

Tutor Tip

To use up fruit cake trimmings, simply mix them with marzipan and a small amount of rum. Dust with cocoa powder to finish.

Cookies

This recipe makes approximately 12–15 dress cookies (see page 183) or 1 rectangular camellia cookie (see page 51).
To make these cookies nice and crispy, beat the butter and sugar together until the mixture becomes very fluffy. I also recommend that you check the cookies whilst they are baking and move them around so that they are evenly baked and do not get burnt.

Ingredients

100g (3½oz) unsalted butter, softened

70g (2½oz) caster sugar

200g (7oz) plain flour, sifted

40g (1½oz) eggs, lightly beaten

Equipment

Electric mixer with paddle attachment

Pair of marzipan spacers

Chopping board

Large rolling pin

Cookie cutters

Small palette knife

Baking tray

Greaseproof paper

Wire cooling rack

25cm x 35cm (10" x 14") food-grade plastic bag

1 Beat the butter and sugar together in an electric mixer with a paddle attachment until light and fluffy.

2 Beat in the eggs one at a time until well mixed. Add the flour and mix on a low speed or with a wooden spoon until it forms a dough.

3 Put the dough in a plastic bag and press the dough together with your hands through the bag (this will prevent your hands from sticking to the dough). Leave to chill in a refrigerator for at least one hour.

4 Place the bag of cookie dough on a chopping board and roll out the dough to an even thickness on top of the bag. Use marzipan spacers to roll the dough to an even thickness of approximately 4mm (¹⁄₆").

5 Chill the dough in the refrigerator again until firm then preheat the oven to 150°C–160°C/300°–325°F/gas mark 2–3.

6 Place the bag of dough back on the board. Cut along two sides of the plastic bag, open it out and cut out the desired shape from the dough with a cookie cutter.

7 Line a baking tray with greaseproof paper and use a palette knife to help you place the cookies onto it.

8 Bake for 15–20 minutes until golden brown at the edges, then leave to cool on a wire rack.

Tutor Tips

Keep the cookie dough inside the plastic bag until you want to cut the dough with the cutters. By doing so you avoid having to flour the board which means your cookies will taste better and your hands won't get as sticky.

I have reduced the amount of caster sugar in this recipe by 30% as I usually ice these cookies. You can add up to 100g (3½oz) more sugar if you are baking cookies that will not be iced.

  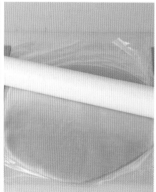 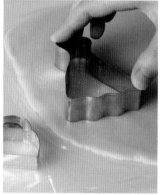

Sugar syrup (moistening syrup)

Sugar syrup can be brushed over a sponge cake with a pastry brush to keep it moist, to add flavour and to make it easier to spread ganache or buttercream over the cake.

Ingredients

30g (1oz) sugar
30ml (1fl oz) water

Equipment

Deep saucepan
Spatula
Airtight container

This recipe makes enough sugar syrup for a 15cm (6") round cake. For every 2cm–3cm (1") increase in the cake size, add 30–50g/ml (1–1¾oz/fl oz) more sugar and water.

1 Place the water and sugar in a deep saucepan and bring to the boil. Stir occasionally to make sure the sugar crystals have dissolved.

2 Remove from the heat and allow it to cool. If you have added liqueur to the syrup, store the syrup before it cools so that it holds the flavour of the liqueur.

3 Store in an airtight container in the fridge for up to three weeks.

To flavour the syrup, add approximately 20ml (4tsp) of brandy, rum or orange liqueur to the syrup mixture before you remove it from the heat to make the alcohol evaporate.

Buttercream

This recipe is rich and creamy, but if you prefer a lighter taste then just add more icing sugar. The basic recipe can be flavoured if required to suit your taste.

Ingredients

250g (8¾oz) butter, softened
250g (8¾oz) icing sugar, sifted
A few drops of vanilla extract

Equipment

Electric mixer with paddle attachment
Container with lid

1 Place the softened butter, icing sugar and vanilla extract into the bowl of an electric mixer fitted with a paddle attachment.

2 Beat together on a low speed until the mixture is well combined, then turn the speed up until the mixture becomes light and fluffy.

3 Store in a sealed container in the fridge for up to 10 days. Bring the buttercream to room temperature before use.

This recipe makes enough buttercream to fill and ice a 15cm (6") round cake. If the cake you are using is bigger, add 100g–200g (3½oz–7oz) of butter and icing sugar for every 2cm–3cm (1") increase in the cake size.

Flavourings

The following quantities make 100g (3½oz) of filling.

Rum raisin

Soak 50g (1¾oz) dried raisins in rum for two weeks prior to making the buttercream. Add the fruit to 50g (1¾oz) buttercream and mix in well. This variation makes a great filling for a chocolate sponge cake and you can use less rum if you want to reduce the alcohol content.

Cherry

Drain and cut 50g (1¾oz) maraschino cherries into quarters. Add them to 50g (1¾oz) buttercream and mix in well.

Raspberry

Add 20g (¾oz) of buttercream to 80g (2¾oz) raspberry jam and mix in well. By adding a small amount of buttercream to the jam, it makes the jam easier to spread over the cake. This filling works well with chocolate cakes.

Rose petal

Add 20g (¾oz) of buttercream to 80g (2¾oz) rose petal jam and mix in well. (If you can't find rose petal jam at the supermarket, recipes are readily available online.) The jam gives the filling a subtle rose flavouring and would complement a cake decorated with roses, such as the English Rose Cake (see page 88).

Tutor Tip

Mix the flavoured ingredients with a small amount of the buttercream filling rather than mixing into the whole quantity of buttercream. This will mean the buttercream remains easy to spread over the surface of the cake, the flavour will be more intense and the filling will keep its freshness. Slice the cake horizontally, spread buttercream on the cake and then layer the flavoured icing on top of it.

Chocolate ganache

Chocolate ganache is a rich, delicious and very versatile filling. When you first make this recipe, the ganache will be very runny but it will slowly start to set. Make sure that you spread the ganache over your cake whilst it is still runny. Once the ganache has set, you can mix it with buttercream to make it easier to spread.

Ingredients

300g (10½oz) dark (semi-sweet) couverture chocolate drops (minimum 53% cocoa solids)

300ml (10½fl oz) single cream

Equipment

Whisk

Wooden spoon

Mixing bowl

Two saucepans (one small and one large) or a double boiler/bain marie pan

1 Place the chocolate drops in a mixing bowl.

2 Bring some water to the boil in one saucepan and then place a smaller saucepan on top of it. Pour the single cream into the saucepan on top. Heat the cream on a low heat and stir well with a wooden spoon once it starts to simmer.

3 Pour the hot cream over the chocolate in the mixing bowl and whisk them together slowly until smooth.

4 Once cool, store the ganache in a sealed container in the fridge for up to three weeks. Bring the ganache to room temperature before use. If you want the ganache to be runny, fill a bowl with hot water, place the ganache in another bowl and place this bowl over the first. Leave for a while, then stir slowly.

Buttercream for piping

Buttercream tastes better when it contains just butter rather than vegetable fat (shortening), however this means that the warmth from your hand will make it too soft to pipe. If you use white vegetable fat the buttercream will keep its shape, but it won't taste as good. When piping with buttercream I use an equal amount of both: the ratio of butter to white vegetable fat in this recipe is a basic guideline which you can adjust to suit your own taste.

Ingredients

50g (1¾oz) salted butter, at room temperature

50g (1¾oz) white vegetable fat (shortening), at room temperature

20ml (¾fl oz) cooled, boiled water

600g (1lb 5¼oz) icing sugar

A few drops of vanilla or peppermint essence (optional)

Equipment

Food mixer or whisk

Bowl

Airtight container

1 Beat the butter and white vegetable fat together until light and fluffy.

2 Beat in the water gradually, until it is all mixed in.

3 Add the icing sugar and beat until light and fluffy again.

4 If you wish, add a few drops of essence to the buttercream at this point and mix well.

5 Keep the buttercream in an airtight container and store in a refrigerator for up to one week.

Sugar Pastes

All the pastes used in sugarcraft mainly consist of icing sugar, white vegetable fat and glucose. It is the varying amounts of those standard ingredients and the addition of any extra gums which make each paste differ in texture and strength. The different types of paste are all readily available from sugarcraft suppliers (see page 196).

Sugarpaste (rolled fondant)

Most sugarpastes contain glycerine, which makes the paste very soft, smooth and ideal for covering cakes. There is a wide range of ready-made coloured sugarpastes available or you can add paste colour to white (see below).

Flower paste (gum paste)

Flower paste is pliable and because it contains gum tragacanth, it is strong enough to roll out very thinly without breaking. It is primarily used to make sugar flowers and leaves. Ready-made coloured flower pastes are available from most sugarcraft suppliers.

Modelling paste
(Mexican paste)

Modelling paste is a mix of both sugarpaste and flower paste; its pliability means that it is ideal for modelling figures, fabrics and other moulded decorations. There are many ready-made modelling pastes on the market but I prefer to mix my own so that I can adjust the strength of the paste to suit the piece I am modelling.

A basic modelling paste should consist of 50% sugarpaste and 50% flower paste. If the paste is too soft and won't hold its shape, add more flower paste; if it is too stiff and difficult to mould, add more sugarpaste to the mix. As the consistency of the paste can be affected by the heat of your hands or the climate you are working in, it is best to adjust the mix of flower paste and sugarpaste each time you use it so that it suits your specific working conditions.

Storage

Always keep any paste you are working with sealed in a food-grade polythene bag to prevent it from drying out. To store, place any leftover paste in a food-grade polythene bag and then place in an airtight container. You can store all pastes in the fridge or freezer, but make sure that you bring the paste to room temperature again before you use it. Pastes can usually be kept for up to a few weeks in the fridge and up to a few months in the freezer, however coloured pastes tend to dry out quicker and should not be left for so long. If you are using ready-made pastes, check the pack for storage guidelines.

Colouring

When colouring pastes it is best to use paste food colours, as liquid food colours can alter the consistency of the paste. To colour, pick up a tiny amount of your chosen paste colour on a cocktail stick and touch it on the sugar paste. Knead the colour into the paste until you achieve an even, consistent colour throughout.

When colouring a large amount of paste, prepare a small ball of intensely coloured paste and knead it into the rest of the paste until it is evenly mixed through. Repeat until the whole piece of paste is coloured.

Dust food colours are used when colouring dry sugar work. Use a dry paintbrush to dust your chosen colour over the work. For a more pronounced effect, mix with a little clear alcohol and paint onto your work; the alcohol will evaporate leaving the colour on the cake.

Edible glue (sugar glue)

Edible glue is ideal for sticking pieces of fresh sugar work together before they dry out. Apply a tiny amount of edible glue with a fine paintbrush to the pieces you want to stick together. Be careful not to use too much glue or the pieces could slide out of position. You can buy ready-made edible glue from sugarcraft suppliers or make your own with the following recipe:

Edibles

15 parts cooled, boiled water

1 part CMC gum (carboxymethyl cellulose)

Equipment

Wooden spoon

Mixing bowl

Airtight container, sterilised

1 Mix 15 parts of cooled, boiled water with 1 part CMC in a mixing bowl.

2 Cover the bowl and then leave the mixture for a day so the CMC has time to dissolve.

3 Store in a sterilised airtight container in the refrigerator for up to a week.

Tutor Tip

If you want to glue dry pieces of sugar work together, you can use a small amount of royal icing or flower paste mixed to a paste with a little cooled, boiled water.

Royal Icing

I have used Instant Mix Royal Icing from Squires Kitchen throughout this book: this is quick and easy to make (see pack instructions) and will give consistent results. If you would like to make your own royal icing I recommend the following basic recipe.

Basic royal icing recipe

Edibles

50g (1¾oz) egg white, at room temperature (I mix 10g (¼oz) powdered albumen and 50ml (1¾floz) cooled, boiled water or you can use free range fresh egg white*)

270g (9½oz) pure icing sugar, sifted (quantity may vary slightly if using fresh egg white)

Equipment

Tea strainer

Electric mixer with paddle attachment

This recipe makes 300g–320g (10½oz–11¼oz) royal icing, approximately enough to fill 12–15 piping bags.

*You can use fresh egg white, however I prefer to use pasteurized, powdered albumen as it will last longer and you can measure it accurately. To reconstitute the albumen, mix 10g (¼oz) of powdered albumen well with 50ml (1¾floz) of cooled, boiled water or follow the instructions on the packet. Leave it for a few hours and then strain through a tea strainer or a small sieve.

The Food Standards Agency recommends using only pasteurised egg in any food that will not be cooked (or only lightly cooked). If you decide to use fresh egg white always use eggs bearing the Lion mark, which guarantees that they have been produced to the highest standards of food safety. All Lion Quality eggs come from British hens vaccinated against salmonella, are fully traceable and have a 'best before' date on the shell as a guarantee of freshness. This is particularly important for cake makers and decorators as you may well use eggs for baking and preparing icings, marzipans and cake fillings.

1 Place the strained egg white and ⅔ of the icing sugar into the bowl of a mixer.

2 Use the paddle attachment to mix it at low speed, until the mixture becomes creamy and shiny.

3 Add the rest of the icing sugar and keep mixing until the icing is stiff enough to hold its shape.

Consistencies

If you want to adjust the consistency of royal icing, either add more icing sugar or more cold water to the royal icing mix.

Soft peak/normal: When you lift the icing with a palette knife, the tip of the

Soft peak/normal

Stiff peak

Firm

Run-out

peak should bend over. This icing should be used with nos. 00–1 and sometimes no. 2 nozzles.

Stiff peak: Add 10g (¼oz) of icing sugar to every 100g (3½oz) of soft-peak royal icing and re-beat. When you lift the icing with a palette knife, it should form stiff peaks. This icing is best for use with: round nozzles sometimes no. 2, usually nos. 3 and over; star nozzle nos. 14 and over; flower and leaf nozzle nos. 101s–101 and no. 67.

Firm: To make your icing even firmer, add 20g (¾oz) of icing sugar to every 100g (3½oz) of soft-peak royal icing and mix well. The consistency should be firm enough to allow piped petals to hold their shape. This icing is best for use with: flower petal nozzle nos. 101 and over and leaf nozzle nos. 67 and 70.

Run-out: Add a few drops of cold, pre-boiled water to soft-peak royal icing and stir well. When you cut into the icing with a palette knife, it should flow back together as follows:

A) After 5 seconds: suitable for flooding larger pieces of work.

B) After 10 seconds: suitable for flooding smaller pieces of work.

C) After 15 seconds: somewhere between soft-peak and run-out icing. This 'loose' icing holds its shape so that you don't have to pipe an outline first. For example,

I have used this 'loose' consistency icing to pipe the dots on the side of the cake in the Christmas Couture Cake project (see page 166), and the rose pattern on the ribbon for the Bird of Joy Cake (see page 156).

Royal icing with corn syrup

(Tropical cake, leaf cookies)

Royal icing with added corn syrup (sometimes known as glucose syrup) is good for creating royal iced designs that include a number of colours, as the extra corn syrup means the icing dries slower than usual. To make royal icing with corn syrup, add 8g (¼oz) of corn syrup to every 100g (3½oz) of soft-peak royal icing and mix in well. Add extra egg white to thin out the icing, or icing sugar to make it thicker.

Storing royal icing

Whilst you are working with royal icing, keep it in a bowl and cover with a clean, damp cloth to prevent it from drying out. It is also helpful to cover any nozzles on piping bags that you are using with a damp cloth, too.

Once you have finished with the royal icing, I recommend that for best results you keep it in a sealed plastic container at room temperature for up to two days. It is important to re-mix the icing before you use it again as it may have separated.

Using colour with royal icing

I use liquid food colour to colour most of my royal icing work. However, I recommend using a small amount of paste food colour if you want to make the icing a deeper colour. Paste food colours that contain glycerine (also known as glycerol) and glycerides should be avoided for royal icing as they will prevent the icing from fully drying. However, it is worth noting that all paste food colours in the Squires Kitchen range do not contain glycerine and are suitable for use with royal icing. When colouring your icing, be careful not to add too much liquid colour or you will alter the consistency of the icing and prevent it from drying. Paste colours should be added a little at a time with a cocktail stick. Make sure that the colour is mixed through thoroughly before use.

How to make a piping bag

Ready-made, reusable piping bags are available but paper piping bags are useful when you only need a small amount of royal icing. I recommend making piping bags from greaseproof paper (see below) as they are suitable for most royal icing work and the paper is waterproof.

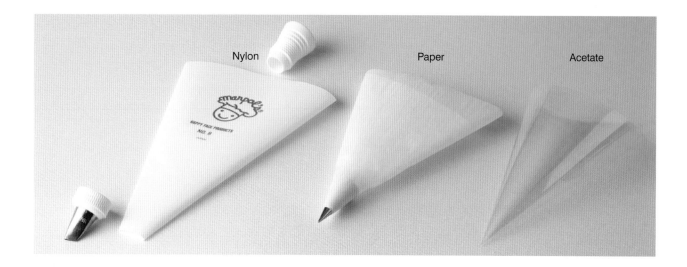

Nylon   Paper   Acetate

Greaseproof piping bag

You will need

Greaseproof paper

Scissors

Tutor Tip

You could make the bag simply by folding a triangular piece of paper but the extra strips give you more paper to wrap around, making the bag stronger.

1 Cut a piece of greaseproof paper to 20cm x 30cm (8" x 12") in size. Fold the paper diagonally at 45°, leaving 6cm (2³⁄₈") strips along the shorter sides of the rectangle. Cut along the folded line using scissors.

2 Make a little fold in the centre of the long side of the triangle. Holding the paper at both ends of the long side, bring the end with the extra strip round to create a point in the middle of the long side of the triangle. Hold this in position then wrap the other side around it.

3 Fold the corners of the bag in at the top, then make two small cuts and fold the middle part in so that the bag holds its shape.

4 Snip 1cm (³⁄₈") off the tip of the bag and drop a nozzle into the hole. Fill the bag just under ½ full with royal icing using a small palette knife. Once the icing is in the bag, fold the top down twice and fold both corners in to seal it.

5 To pipe, hold the bag as you would hold a pencil and gently squeeze out the icing, supporting your wrist with the other hand.

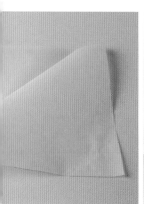

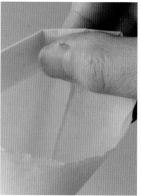

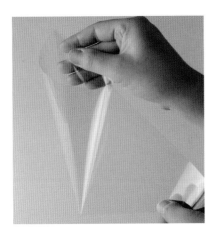

Acetate piping bag

This bag is particularly good for piping dots, simple lines and run-out work without a nozzle, as the sheet is strong enough to hold its shape. It means that you don't need to wash any nozzles and, as the bag is transparent, you can easily differentiate between bags if you are working with several different colours of icing at once. When buying acetate for a piping bag, make sure you choose a thicker sheet (0.4mm or more) so that the bag is strong enough to hold the icing.

You will need

25cm (10") acetate square
Scissors
Sticky tape

1 To make a 13cm x 9cm (5¼" x 3½") piping bag you will need a sheet of acetate that is 25cm (10") square. Cut the acetate sheet in half to make a triangle.

2 Wrap the sheet into a cone in the same way as for the greaseproof paper piping bag (see step 2, opposite).

3 Secure the bag by taping it on the outside at the top (pointed end) and on the inside at the top.

4 Place some royal icing into the bag to just under ½ full. Fold the open end over a few times and secure with tape.

5 When you are ready to pipe, snip the tip off the end of the bag to the size required.

6 To pipe, hold the bag as you would hold a pencil and gently squeeze out the icing.

Nylon piping bag

Nylon piping bags are suitable for piping flowers with firm-peak royal icing and won't tear whilst you are piping. A plastic coupler ring allows you to change the nozzle in the piping bag without having to make up a new bag of icing. This is good if you want to use exactly the same colour royal icing for a different piece of work. Different size bags and coupler rings are available, but 20cm (8") and 12.5cm (5") are the most commonly used sizes in sugarcraft. Choose the coupler ring to fit your nozzle.

You will need

Nylon piping bag
Scissors
Piping nozzle with coupler

1 Snip 1cm (³/₈") off the end of the bag and place the coupler into the bag. Attach the nozzle and then the ring from the coupler from the outside of the bag and secure all three together by twisting the ring.

2 Use a palette knife to fill the bag to just under ½ full with firm royal icing, twist and close the end of the bag.

3 Hold the bag as you would hold a pencil and use your thumb to squeeze out the icing.

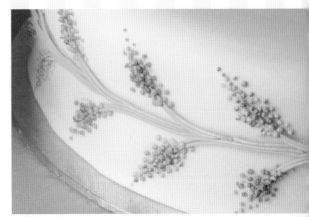

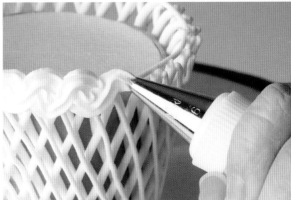

Piping with royal icing

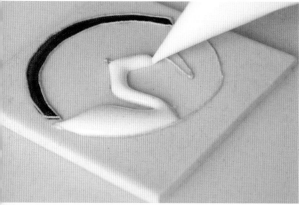

Run-out work

When flooding a piece of work with run-out icing, make sure you use enough icing to flood the whole piece as it will lose height once it dries out. Be careful not to use too much icing, however, as you don't want it to flow over the piped outline. If you spot any air bubbles on the surface of the icing, use a sterilised dress pin to prick them as soon as you find them. To achieve a professional finish, you can help the icing to dry out quicker by leaving the work in a dehydrator (available from Squires Kitchen) or under a desk lamp.

1 Use a no. 0 nozzle and soft-peak royal icing to pipe an outline around the area you would like to flood.

2 Fill the bag to just under ½ full with run-out icing and fold down the open end tightly so that the icing does not leak out of the top whilst you are piping.

3 To flood a narrow space, you can either snip the tip off the end of a paper piping bag or prepare a piping bag with a no. 1, 1.5 or 2 nozzle. To flood a larger space, you will need a no. 3 or 4 nozzle.

4 First, flood the icing gently just inside the outline and then fill in the rest of the space without stopping. Fill any gaps by pressing out and smoothing down the icing with a damp, thin paintbrush.

Line work

It is best to use either soft-peak or stiff-peak royal icing for line work. Before you place the icing in a piping bag, paddle the royal icing with a palette knife to eliminate any air bubbles as they will cause breaks and holes in your piping work.

Piping a straight line: Hold your piping bag at a 60° angle, touch the tip of the nozzle to the starting point and gently squeeze out the icing. Lift the bag whilst you are squeezing so you can see the line you are piping and continue the line straight towards the finishing point. Try not to let the line sag down. Release the pressure when you want to stop and bring the nozzle down to the finish point. You can achieve a straight line by keeping the pressure constant on the piping bag.

Piping curved lines: In the same way as for a straight line, squeeze out the icing slower and lift the bag lower than when piping a straight line as you work.

Pressure piping

Pressure piping is a technique that is used to create three-dimensional designs with royal icing. By increasing and decreasing the amount of pressure on the bag you can create a variety of 3-D designs, from small dots to flowers, animals and scrolls. Once you have piped your shape reduce the pressure and stop squeezing gradually. The consistency of the royal icing you need for this work depends on the size of the nozzle you use; the smaller the nozzle, the softer the icing should be.

Brush embroidery

Brush embroidery is a technique that involves pressure piping directly onto a cake or an acetate sheet. Once you have marked out your design, pressure pipe around the outline and then use a damp brush to stroke the icing towards the centre before the icing is dry. This technique is usually used for ornate flowers and leaves, as the brushstrokes resemble the veins.

Piping Flowerets

Materials

Stiff- or firm-peak royal icing

Equipment

Piping bag
Piping nozzle nos.: 101s, 101
Flower nail
Greaseproof paper cut into small squares

Flowerets

1 Attach a small square of greaseproof paper to a flower nail with a small amount of royal icing.

2 Hold the bag with your dominant hand and the flower nail in your other hand. Hold the bag at an angle of 45° and place the thicker part of the nozzle onto the nail. Pipe petals from the outside toward the centre as you turn the nail.

3 Take the paper off the nail once you have finished piping. Once it dries, remove the flower from the paper and secure it in place with royal icing.

Four-petal and five-petal flowers

1 Repeat step 1 as above.

2 Hold the bag with your dominant hand and the flower nail in your other hand. For a four-petal flower, pipe a petal with each ¼ rotation of the flower nail and finish four petals in one rotation. To pipe a five-petal flower, pipe a petal with each $1\frac{1}{5}$ rotation of the flower nail.

3 Repeat step 3 as above.

Covering cakes with marzipan and sugarpaste

Preparing the cakes for covering

The quantities given here are for a 15cm (6") round sponge or fruit cake. See page 19 for guidance on how much filling is required for larger sponge cakes.

Edibles

15cm (6") round sponge or fruit cake

For a 15cm (6") sponge cake:

500g (1lb 1¾oz) buttercream (see page 19)

60g (2oz) sugar syrup (optional, see page 19)

For a 15cm (6") fruit cake (see page 32):

Apricot jam

A small amount of water

A small amount of caster sugar

A small amount of marzipan (taken from the main quantity for the cake covering)

Equipment

15cm (6") round cake board

Turntable

Greaseproof paper

Large serrated knife

Small sharp knife

Large and small palette knives

Pastry brush

Cotton thread or cake leveller

Non-stick board

Cocktail sticks

Sponge cake

1 Using a serrated knife, cut off the dome from the top of the sponge cake (if the cake has one) to make the surface of the cake flat and level.

> ### Tutor Tip
>
> It is best to use a small spirit level to ensure that your cakes are level, rather than simply judging by eye. Place a spare cake board on top of the cake so the spirit level doesn't come into direct contact with the cake

2 Place a sheet of greaseproof paper and the 15cm (6") cake board onto the turntable (this will make the cake easier to move once covered). Put a tiny amount of buttercream filling onto the cake board to act as a glue.

3 Slice the sponge cake into four equal layers that are about 2cm (¾") deep. You can do this using a cake leveller or with a long piece of cheese wire as follows:

- Insert four cocktail sticks evenly spaced around the cake, each at ¼ of the way up from the bottom of the cake.

- Use a piece of cheese wire that is at least 20cm (8") longer than the circumference of the cake. Wind it tightly around the cake at the height of the cocktail sticks.

- Cross the ends of the wire, hold them in your hands and pull it in one go to slice through the cake.

- Slice the cake in the same way at the halfway point and ¾ up the sides of the cake.

4 Place the first sponge layer onto the cake board on the turntable. If desired, you can brush each layer of cake with sugar syrup before spreading the buttercream to keep the cake moist. Spread buttercream and jam over the top of the cake with a palette knife and place the second layer of sponge on top. Continue in the same way with all the layers of the cake until it is assembled.

5 To crumb-coat the cake, use a large palette knife to spread a thin, even layer of buttercream over the top of the cake. Rotate the turntable and cover the sides of the cake thinly with buttercream, too. This coating of buttercream will seal the cake and prevent any crumbs from getting into the marzipan or sugarpaste covering.

6 Carefully remove the cake from the turntable by holding the greaseproof paper underneath and keep it in the refrigerator until the buttercream firms up. Tidy up the coating with a large palette knife and chill it again; when the cake feels firm it is ready to be covered with marzipan and/or sugarpaste.

Fruit cake

1 Using a serrated knife, cut away the top of the fruit cake to make a flat and level surface. Fill any holes in the fruit cake with small pieces of marzipan.

2 Put a tiny amount of royal icing on the cake board to act as a glue, then place the cake on the board.

3 Bring some apricot jam to the boil with a small amount of water and caster sugar. Leave it to cool for a minute. Use a pastry brush or palette knife to spread a thin layer of apricot glaze over the cake.

Covering cakes with marzipan and sugarpaste

Covering a cake

The quantities given here are enough to cover a 15cm (6") round sponge or fruit cake. A table of quantities for different sized cakes is given on page 29.

Edibles

15cm (6") sponge or fruit cake, prepared opposite

500g (1lb 1¾oz) marzipan

500g (1lb 1¾oz) sugarpaste

Icing (confectioners') sugar

Equipment

Cake board the same size and shape as the cake

Side scraper

Large rolling pin

2 marzipan spacers

2 cake smoothers

Small, sharp knife or pizza wheel

Tea strainer or small sieve

Non-stick board

Tutor Tips

You should always cover a fruit cake with a layer of marzipan before you cover it with sugarpaste, but you can cover sponge cakes with two layers of sugarpaste if you prefer. Covering the cake twice gives the cake a nicer shape.

If the cake board is slightly larger than the cake, cover the cake with marzipan to the top of the cake board and trim neatly. Bring the sugarpaste to the bottom of the cake board to cover it completely.

Covering a round cake

1 Once you have prepared your cake as explained on pages 30 to 32, cover it with marzipan (optional for sponge cakes) following the steps for sugarpaste below. Brush the surface with a little clear alcohol to help the sugarpaste stick.

2 Knead the required amount of sugarpaste (or marzipan) on a non-stick board until it is smooth and pliable. Sprinkle a little icing sugar on the board if the paste becomes too sticky.

3 Use a tea strainer or a small sieve to dust your work surface with icing sugar and roll out the sugarpaste. When rolling the paste ensure to keep moving it around so that it does not stick to the work surface. Remember, however, that you should not turn the paste over as the underside will be covered with icing sugar.

4 Roll it out to an even, round shape that is large enough to cover the top and sides of the cake in one go. To work out how big the paste needs to be, multiply the height of the cake by 1½–2 (depending on how deep the cake is) and add this to the diameter of the cake. Use marzipan spacers to help you roll out the paste to an even thickness.

Tutor Tip

The thickness of the marzipan covering should be approximately 3mm (1/8") and the thickness of the sugarpaste should be 5mm (3/16"). The sugarpaste is usually rolled out slightly thicker as it will become thinner once it is smoothed out over the cake.

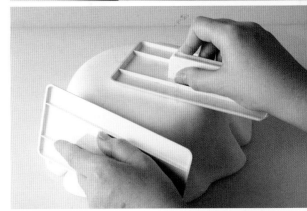

5 Place the rolling pin in the middle of the rolled paste and gently fold the paste over the pin. Lift the paste with the rolling pin and lay it over the centre of the cake.

6 Use the palms of your hands to smooth the paste across the top and down the sides of the cake to remove any unwanted air bubbles. Repeat this step using cake smoothers instead of your hands to achieve a neater, polished finish.

7 Trim away any excess marzipan or sugarpaste from around the base with either a pizza wheel or a small, sharp knife to make a neat edge. To finish, neaten around the base of the cake with a side scraper.

Covering shapes with corners

1 To cover a square cake or any other shape with corners, follow steps 1–5 for covering a round cake above.

2 After you have placed the marzipan and/or sugarpaste onto the cake, press the paste down with your palms and fit it to the corners of the cake. Smooth the sides of the cake from the top downwards with your palms and then with the cake smoothers. It is important to start with the corners and work down, otherwise the paste will gather at the corners.

Covering a cake: straight-edge finish

1 Roll out the marzipan or sugarpaste on a work surface dusted with icing sugar, making sure that it is bigger than the top of the cake that you want to cover. Place either the cake or the cake tin you used to bake it in onto the paste to use as a template. Use a sharp knife to cut around the cake or tin so that you are left with a piece of paste that is the same size and shape as the top of your cake. Brush the top of the cake with buttercream (for sponge cakes) or apricot glaze (for fruit cakes) then place this paste on top of the cake and smooth out towards the edges using a cake smoother.

2 Wrap a long strip of greaseproof paper around the sides of the cake and cut to size. Roll out the marzipan or sugarpaste into a long strip to a thickness of about 4mm (just over $1/8$"). Cut the paste to size using the paper template, dust a small amount of icing sugar onto the strip to prevent it sticking together and roll it up loosely from one end.

3 Attach one end of the rolled paste to the cake and unroll it slowly around the sides of the cake. Smooth down the paste with the cake smoothers and trim away any excess to make a neat join.

Tutor Tips

Covering the top and sides of the cake separately means you can achieve a sharp top edge.

For a larger cake, make two or three strips of paste the same size and unroll them around the cake separately. Smooth the joins together with your fingers and a cake smoother.

Quantities for covering cakes with sugarpaste and marzipan

As a general rule of thumb, approximately 20% of the sugarpaste and marzipan used would be left over after covering a cake. If you are covering two or more cakes at a time (e.g. for a tiered wedding cake), you can reduce the sugarpaste and marzipan quantities for the smaller tiers by approximately 20% (i.e. a fifth) when calculating how much to buy.

Approx. depth 7.5cm (3")	10cm (4")	15cm (6")	18cm (7")	20cm (8")	23cm (9")	25cm (10")	28cm (11")	30cm (12")
Round	400g (14oz)	500g (1lb 1¾oz)	600g (1lb 5¼oz)	800g (1lb 12oz)	900g (2lb)	1.2kg (2lb 10¼oz)	1.4kg (3lb½oz)	1.7kg (3lb 12oz)
Square	500g (1lb 1¾oz)	600g (1lb 5¼oz)	700g (1lb 8¾oz)	900g (2lb)	1.2kg (2lb 10¼oz)	1.4kg (3lb 1½oz)	1.7kg (3lb 12oz)	1.8kg (4lb)

Covering a cake drum/board with sugarpaste

The quantity of sugarpaste given here is for a 25cm (10") cake drum. See below for guidance on how much sugarpaste is required for different sized boards.

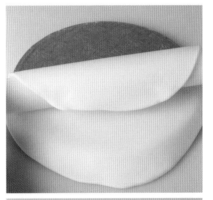

Edibles

800g (1lb 12oz) sugarpaste for cake drum

A small amount of cooled, boiled water

Equipment

25cm (10") cake drum

Large rolling pin

Small sharp knife

Pastry brush

1 Use a pastry brush to brush the cake drum with a small amount of cooled, boiled water.

2 Knead the sugarpaste and then roll it out until it is approximately 5mm (³/₁₆") thick and the size of the cake drum you want to cover. Fold the paste over a large rolling pin and lay it over the cake drum.

3 Roll over the paste with a rolling pin to secure it to the cake drum and to remove any air bubbles.

4 Holding the drum in one hand, carefully use a sharp knife to trim any excess sugarpaste from around the edge and leave it to dry for a few days.

Quantities for covering a cake drum/board with sugarpaste

	20cm (8")	25cm (10")	28cm (11")	30cm (12")	33cm (13")	35cm (14")	38cm (15")	40cm (16")	46cm (18")	48cm (19")
Round or square	650g (1lb 7oz)	820g (1lb 13oz)	850g (1lb 14oz)	870g (1lb 15oz)	900g (2lb)	930g (2lb 1oz)	950g (2lb 1½oz)	1kg (2lb 3¼oz)	1.2kg (2lb 10¼oz)	1.5kg (3lb 5oz)

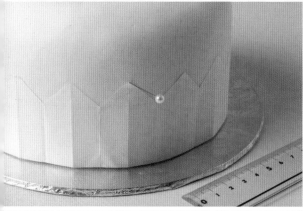

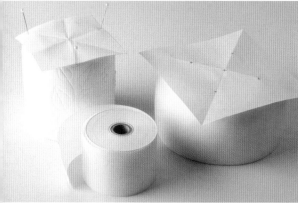

Making and using paper templates

This paper template is simple to use and works with cakes of any size and shape. You can make accurate marks on the cake by attaching the template to the cake with cocktail sticks or sterilised dress pins.

Making a paper dowelling template

Equipment

Greaseproof paper

Scissors

Ruler

Pencil

Cocktail sticks

Dress pins (sterilised in alcohol)

Tutor Tip

It is important to find the centre point of the paper template.

1 Cut a square of greaseproof paper to the same size as the cake. Fold the paper in half and then in half again to find the centre, then open out. These folds in the paper allow you to divide the cake equally into quarters and any multiples of four. If you want to divide the cake equally into three or any multiples of three, fold the paper from the centre point into three (the angle at the folded point should be 60°). Open out the paper.

2 Measure the radius of the tier above from the central point of the cake. Mark along the fold lines approximately two thirds of the cake radius from the centre of the paper template.

To make a dowelling template for a cake which is stacked off-centre (such as the Christmas Couture Cake on pages 166 to 177), follow a slightly different method as follows:

1 Fold a square of greaseproof paper into quarters as before, to find the centre.

2 Measure the length of how much you would like to offset the centre of the second tier from the first one. Then mark a point of that length onto a crease from the centre of the paper using a pencil and a ruler.

3 Fold the paper at a right angle (90°) at the marked point and use this as the point from which you will measure the dowel positions.

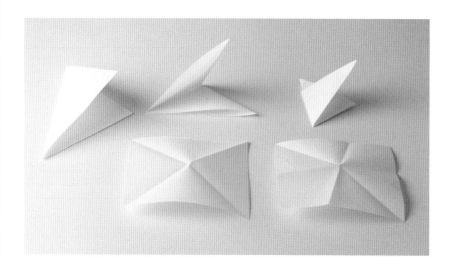

Marking the cake

Edibles

Cake, prepared and covered with sugarpaste (see pages 30 to 35)

A small amount of royal icing

Equipment

Cake template (see opposite)

Dress pins (sterilised in alcohol)

Cocktail sticks

Greaseproof paper

Piping nozzle: no. 0

Scriber (optional)

Marking the top of a cake

1 Place the template on the cake and align the centre of the template with the centre of the cake.

2 Insert cocktail sticks or sterilised dress pins at two points to secure the template in place. Mark where you want the dowels or cake decoration to be, then remove the template and pins from the cake.

3 Use a no. 0 nozzle and royal icing the same colour as the cake to fill the holes that the pins or cocktail sticks have left.

Marking the side of the cake

1 Wrap a strip of greaseproof paper around the circumference of the cake and cut to size.

2 Fold the paper to divide it into equal parts, then wrap it back around the cake and make marks at the creases with a scriber, cocktail stick or sterilised dress pin.

Tutor Tip

So as not to spoil the appearance of the finished cake, it is best to use dress pins sterilised in alcohol to mark out any parts of the cake that will be visible when the whole piece is assembled. Dress pins will leave smaller, neater holes in the cake than a cocktail stick, but cocktail sticks are better if you need to make clear, obvious marks. Always remember to remove any pins or cocktail sticks afterwards and store them safely away from the cake.

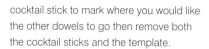

Assembling tiered cakes

If you are making a stacked wedding cake, the lower tiers will need to be supported with dowels to support the weight of the upper tiers. This is particularly important for cakes with three or more tiers.

Dowelling and stacking a tiered cake

There are two kinds of cake dowels: solid (plastic and wooden) and hollow (plastic). I usually use solid plastic dowels as they are light and easy to cut, although hollow dowels will work just as well. Wooden dowels are only used to support heavier cakes. You should use a minimum of 3–4 dowels per cake and can add more depending on the weight of the cake on the next tier and the number of tiers above it. When positioning the dowels, make sure they are placed so that they will effectively support the next tier. Make the dowel template on page 36 and use as a guide.

Edibles

Cakes, prepared and covered with sugarpaste, on cake cards of the same size

A sugar flower bouquet

A small amount of royal icing

Clear alcohol or boiling water

Equipment

Sugarpasted cake drum

Large rolling pin

Craft knife

Cake dowels

Dowel template, see page 36

Pencil

Cocktail sticks

1 Put a small amount of royal icing in the centre of the sugarpasted cake drum and secure the bottom tier in place.

2 Place your dowelling template on the cake and align the centre of the cake with the centre of the template. Insert a cocktail stick into the centre and another in one other dowelling point, so that the template does not move. Use another cocktail stick to mark where you would like the other dowels to go then remove both the cocktail sticks and the template.

3 Sterilise all dowels before you use them by rubbing them with clear alcohol or placing them in boiling water. Leave them to dry before use.

4 Push the first dowel all the way down to the bottom of the cake and mark with a pencil where the dowel protrudes from the cake, making sure the pencil does not come into contact with the cake covering. Remove the dowel and use a craft knife to cut 1mm ($^1/_{32}$") above the mark.

5 Use this dowel as a guide to cut the other three dowels to exactly the same length and then insert them into the cake at the marked places.

Tutor Tip

It is a good idea to make sure that the dowels are level at this point. You can do so by placing a cake board on top of them and then checking them with a small spirit level.

6 Put a small amount of royal icing in the centre of the dowelled cake, then use both hands to carefully place the next tier on top. If you are stacking three or more tiers, follow the same procedure to dowel all the cakes, excluding the very top tier.

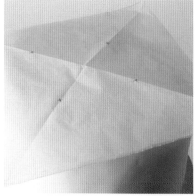

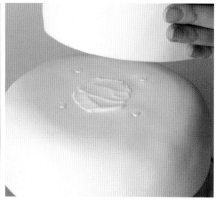

Attaching ribbons

Edibles

Small amount of royal icing

Equipment

Satin ribbon, as long as the circumference/sides of the cake or drum/board plus an extra 2.5cm (1") overlap

Non-toxic glue stick

Double-sided tape (optional)

For a cake drum

Cut a length of 1.5cm (5/8") wide ribbon slightly longer than the circumference of the cake drum. Put glue around the edge of the drum with a non-toxic glue stick and attach the ribbon around the drum. Stick down the ends with a non-toxic glue stick or double-sided tape at the back of the drum. Make sure the glue and tape do not come into contact with the sugarpaste covering.

For a cake

Cut a length of ribbon slightly longer than the circumference of the cake then wrap it around the base of the cake. Stick one end of the ribbon to the cake with a small amount of royal icing, put some icing onto the other end and stick it on top.

Covering cakes with marzipan and sugarpaste

PROJECTS

Camellia Cake

(JANUARY)

Edibles

3 x square cakes:

23cm (9") x 12cm (5") deep for bottom tier

18cm (7") x 10cm (4") deep for middle tier

15cm (6") x 10cm (4") deep (or dummy cake) for top tier

3.05kg (6lb 11½oz) marzipan (SK)

3.05kg (6lb 11½oz) sugarpaste/rolled fondant: white (SK)

500g (1lb 5¼oz) SK Instant Mix Royal Icing: 400g (14oz) coloured red (with Poinsettia and a touch of Cyclamen), 100g (3½oz) white

SK Professional Liquid Food Colours: Cyclamen, Poinsettia

SK Designer Metallic Lustre Dust Food Colour: Light Gold

Clear alcohol

Equipment

Basic equipment (see pages 6 to 7)

20.5cm, 15cm, 13cm (8", 6", 5") square cake boards

Piping nozzles: nos. 0, 1.5

Pliers

Paintbrushes: nos. 0 (fine), 10 (flat) (SK)

Template (page 193)

Rope-effect ribbon: gold

Decoration

Camellia sprays with Tama kanzashi hairpin decoration (see pages 46 to 49)

Covering the cakes

1 Cut away the four corners of the 23cm (9") cake: measure 2.5cm (1") along from each corner, mark two points and cut along the line connecting the two.

2 Position the cake on the 20.5cm (8") square cake board and stick down with royal icing. Cover the cake with 1.4kg (3lb ¼oz) marzipan, then with 1.4kg (3lb ¼oz) white sugarpaste (see pages 30 to 35) and leave the cake to stand overnight.

3 Insert four cake dowels into the cake to support the upper tiers (see page 38).

4 For the middle tier, cut away the four corners of the 18cm (7") cake as before, however this time measure 2cm (¾") from the corners. Attach the cake onto the 15cm (6") square cake board with royal icing. Cover the cake with 900g (1lb 15¾oz) marzipan, then with 900g (1lb 15¾oz) white sugarpaste and leave the cake to dry overnight. Insert the cake dowels as before (see page 38).

5 For the top tier, cut away the corners of the 15cm (6") cake as for the middle tier. Depending on how many guests you are catering for, you may wish to use a polystyrene dummy cake for the top tier. Position the cake on the 13cm (5") square cake board and stick down with royal icing. Cover the cake with 750g (1lb 10½oz) marzipan, then with 750g (1lb 10½oz) white sugarpaste and leave the cake to dry overnight.

Piped camellia design

Tutor Tip

When deciding where to position the camellia patterns, imagine the cake as a finished piece.

6 Lay a piece of tracing paper over the camellia pattern template and trace over it carefully with a pencil. Wipe a dress pin with alcohol to sterilise it, then use it to attach the tracing paper to the cake with the traced side facing out (so that the pencil lines don't touch the cake). Copy the pattern onto the cake by tracing over the pencil line with a skewer or a cocktail stick then remove the template.

7 Fit a piping bag with a no. 0 nozzle and fill with royal icing coloured red (using Poinsettia and a touch of Cyclamen). Pipe over the marked lines on the cake. Pipe vertical lines in the centre of the flowers with dots at the end for the stamens.

Tutor Tip

Gently erase any unwanted lines with a fine paintbrush soaked in a little alcohol.

Brush embroidery

8 Fit a piping bag with a no. 1.5 nozzle and pressure pipe along the edges of the petals with red royal icing. Before the royal icing dries, place a damp, flat paintbrush onto the edge of the petals and stroke the icing in towards the centre of the flower.

Tutor Tip

Royal icing will not brush out smoothly if it is too dry, so pressure pipe along the petal edges in small sections at a time. Always start with the petals in the background, working towards the foreground to create perspective.

9 Fit a piping bag with a no. 0 nozzle and fill with white royal icing. Pipe vertical lines at the flower's centre and pipe dots at the end of these lines. When these dots are dry, paint them with Gold dust food colour dissolved in clear alcohol.

10 Once the decoration is dry, stack the three tiers together and secure with royal icing. As the base cake has no cake board, present the cake on a stand.

Assembly

11 Make the camellia flowers, Rikyuso (stemona japonica) leaves and Tama kanzashi (hairpin decoration) following the instructions on pages 46 to 49. Make

Tutor Tip

When you have assembled the cake, take a good look at the overall piece. Pipe any extra camellia patterns onto the sides of the cake if necessary to balance the overall design.

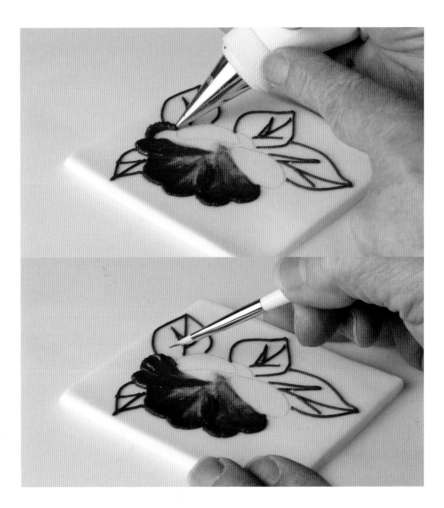

one large and two smaller flower sprays by binding the camellia flowers, buds and leaves together with floral tape. Place three posy picks towards the back of the top tier cake. Make three U-shaped pins from a 20-gauge wire.

12 Arrange the sprays so that the large spray is at the top and the smaller sprays are to the sides. Hold the stems together with the U-shaped pins and secure them into the picks. Arrange the leaves and secure in a posy pick.

13 Fold a gold rope ribbon several times to make loops and secure with a twisted wire. Trim the wire, leaving 3cm (1^1/$_8$") at the end. Arrange the rope ribbon and a Tama kanzashi hairpin as desired (see page 49) and secure with a pick.

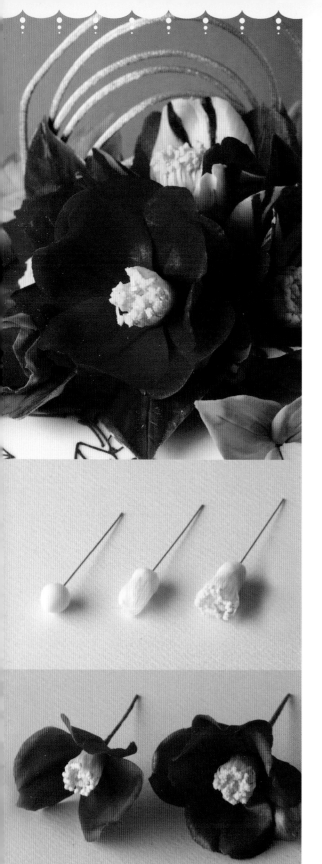

Camellia Sprays

Edibles

SK Sugar Florist Paste (SFP): Cream, Holly/Ivy, Pale Green, Pale Yellow, Poinsettia, White

SK Instant Mix Royal Icing coloured with Daffodil

Small amount of red sugarpaste (SK)

SK Professional Liquid Food Colour: Daffodil

SK Professional Dust Food Colours: Cyclamen, Holly/Ivy, Poinsettia, Vine

SK Designer Dust Food Colour: Jet Black

SK Designer Bridal Satin Lustre Dust Food Colour: White Satin

SK Designer Metallic Lustre Dust Food Colour: Classic Gold

SK Designer Pollen Style Edible Dust Food Colour: Pale Yellow

SK Edible Glue

SK Confectioners' Glaze

Clear alcohol

Equipment

Basic equipment (see page 8)

20-, 24-, 26-, 30-, 32-gauge floral wires: green

20-, 30-gauge floral wires: white

Floral tape: green (half-width and full-width)

Piping nozzle: no. 0

2cm (¾") diameter polystyrene rose centre

2cm (¾") diameter polystyrene ball

Rose petal cutter: 4cm x 5cm (1½" x 2") (Tinkertech)

Rose cutter set (calyces and buds): 4/5 (3.2cm x 3.5cm) and 3/5 (2.7cm x 3cm) (FMM)

For Rikyuso (stemona japonica) leaves:

Large peony petal cutter: 5cm x 3.5cm (2" x 1³/₈") (Tinkertech)

Medium rose petal cutter: 4cm x 2.5cm (1½" x 1") (PME)

Small rose petal cutter: 3.5cm x 2cm (1³/₈" x ¾") (PME)

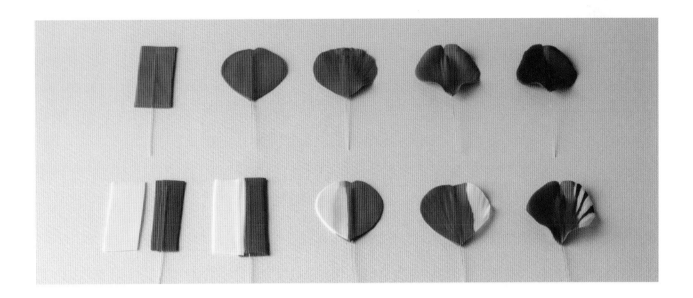

Flower centre

1 Roll a ball of White SFP into a teardrop shape approximately 1cm x 1.5cm ($^3/_8$" x $^5/_8$") in size. Cover a hooked 24-gauge green wire with edible glue, insert it into the bottom of the teardrop and allow to dry.

2 Roll out some Cream SFP into two thin rectangles 2.5cm x 4cm (1" x 1½") in size. Lay them out horizontally and dust with White Satin dust food colour. Use a cutting wheel to make thin, neat cuts all along one side of the paste. Cut about $^2/_3$ into the paste and once finished, bend the fronds of paste inwards. Stick the first rectangle around the White SFP teardrop with edible glue, first attaching it at the bottom of the teardrop and then fitting it to the rounded shape.

3 Follow the same steps with the second rectangle of Cream SFP and attach it to the flower centre so that it sits a little higher than the first. Smooth out the base with your fingers. Before the centre dries out, colour some royal icing with Daffodil liquid food colour and pipe dots at the tips of the

paste using a no. 0 piping nozzle. Dust the tips with with Pale Yellow edible pollen.

Petals

Follow the same process for making both the red petals and the red and white petals.

4 Roll out some Poinsettia SFP and insert a 30-gauge white wire covered with edible glue. Thinly roll out the paste around the wire and cut out a rose petal using a cutter. Cut out a small v-shape from the tip of the petal with a 4/5 rose cutter and use a bamboo skewer or veiner to add veins to the petal. Dust the petals with Poinsettia dust food colour mixed with a little Cyclamen food colour, then use your fingers to bring together the cut edges of the v-shape to give the petal shape. Repeat this step to make seven petals.

5 Before they dry out, arrange the petals around the flower centre and secure them with floral tape. Attach three petals first and then attach the remaining four outside these.

Calyces

6 Make a small ball of Pale Green SFP, brush a little edible glue on one end and insert the wired flower. Thinly roll out some more Pale Green SFP and cut out six calyces with a 4/5 rose cutter, then add veins to each calyx with a corn husk or a veiner. Smooth the edges with a flower shaper and cup with a ball tool (see page 186). Use edible glue to

attach three calyces around the ball of green paste, then attach another three between the first calyces. Dust with Pale Yellow and Vine dust food colours, then dust a little Poinsettia dust food colour on the edges.

Leaves

7 Roll out some Holly/Ivy SFP, leaving a mound for the wire. Cover a 26-gauge green wire with edible glue and insert it into the SFP. Thinly roll out the paste around the wire, turn a rose cutter upside down and cut out a leaf shape. Enlarge the leaf a little with a CelPin, add veins using a veiner and smooth the edge with a flower shaping tool. To finish, pinch the neck of the leaf with your fingers, dust with Holly/Ivy dust and brush with confectioners' glaze (see page 187). Make several leaves in the same way.

Buds

8 Use a polystyrene rose centre that is 2cm (¾") in diameter or make a centre of the same size from SFP. Insert a glued,

hooked 24-gauge wire into the bottom of the polystyrene or SFP and leave to dry (see page 185, how to attach wire to polystyrene).

9 Thinly roll out some Poinsettia SFP and cut out three petals with a 4/5 rose cutter. Add veins with a bamboo skewer and smooth the edges with a bone tool. Glue the petals tightly around the polystyrene centre so that it is completely hidden.

10 Thinly roll out some more Poinsettia SFP and cut out four petals with a 3/5 rose cutter. Cut out a v-shape from the tip of each petal with a 4/5 rose cutter, then add veins and smooth the edges. Be sure to pinch and pleat the bottom of each petal to prevent it from opening. Trim away any excess paste, arrange the petals around the centre and attach to the first petals with edible glue.

11 Mix some Pale Yellow and Pale Green SFP. Thinly roll out the paste and cut out four calyx shapes with a 4/5 rose cutter and three with a 3/5 rose cutter. Add veins with a corn husk or a veiner, smooth the edges with a bone tool and cup them with a ball tool. Make seven altogether.

12 Use edible glue to attach four calyces to the back of the petals and attach three more behind those. Dust with Vine dust food colour and add a little Poinsettia dust at the edges.

Rikyuso

(Stemona japonica)

13 Thinly roll out some Pale Green SFP. Leave a mound at the centre for a wire, then roll out even more thinly. Cut out with an inverted large, medium or small rose cutter and trim the width of the leaf a little with a cutting wheel. Insert a glued, green 30-gauge wire into the mound, add veins with a leaf shaper and soften the edges. Dust the leaf with Vine dust food colour.

14 Tape the wire with green floral tape then bend the wire to 90° at the base of the leaf. Repeat these steps to make 3–5 more leaves in different sizes.

15 Using floral tape, alternately attach 3–5 leaves to a 24-gauge wire, starting with the smallest first. Wind a green

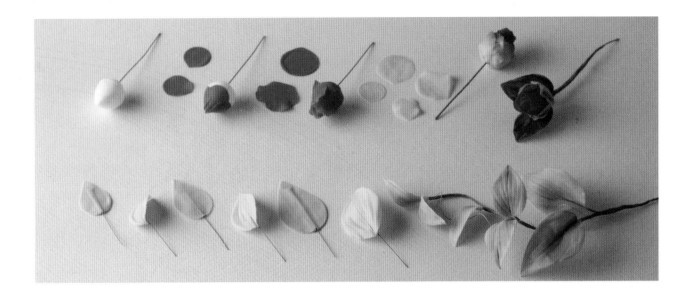

32-gauge wire around a paintbrush to curl it, then intertwine it with the wired leaves.

Tama kanzashi

(Hairpin decoration)

16 Mix together equal amounts of red sugarpaste and Poinsettia SFP and roll a small piece to make a rugby ball shape. Insert a lightly glued 20-gauge white wire through the ball, place it on the board and use your palm to roll it along the wire to

10cm (4") in length. Leave approximately 4cm (1½") of the wire sticking out at both ends, trim the excess and leave to dry.

17 Using a skewer, make a hole through the centre of a 2cm (¾") diameter polystyrene ball. Roll out some of the red paste, cover the ball and push the skewer back through the hole. Remove the skewer and leave it to dry.

18 Insert the wire made in step 16 through the hole in the ball. Brush a little glue over the wire that is left sticking

out and cover with a small square of red paste, smoothing the join with your fingers. Leave to dry.

19 Brush confectioners' glaze over the Tama kanzashi and leave it to dry. Dissolve Gold and Black dust food colours in clear alcohol and paint small flowers and leaves onto the red paste with a fine paintbrush.

Camellia Cookies

Edibles

Cookie dough (see page 16)

300g (10½oz) sugarpaste: white (SK)

SK Instant Mix Royal Icing coloured red (with Poinsettia and a touch of Cyclamen)

SK Professional Liquid Food Colours: Cyclamen, Poinsettia

Equipment

Basic equipment (see pages 6 to 7)

25cm x 35cm (10" x 14") food-grade plastic bag

Baking parchment

Tracing paper

Baking tray

Piping nozzle: no. 0

Template (see page 194)

1 Put some cookie dough in a plastic bag about 25cm x 35cm (10" x 14") in size. Roll out flat with a rolling pin and let it sit in the refrigerator for approximately one hour, or until the dough becomes firm.

2 Once firm, remove the bag from the refrigerator. Cut open two sides of the plastic bag, pull out the dough and place it onto a board covered with baking parchment. The top of the dough should still be covered with plastic.

3 Draw around the template on tracing paper and place the patterned tracing paper onto the plastic bag and trace around it with a quilting tool. Place the dough back into the refrigerator until it

becomes firm enough to cut, then remove and cut along the pattern.

4 Place each part of the cookie separately on a baking tray. Bake for about 20 minutes in an oven preheated to 170°C/340°F/gas mark 3.

5 Roll out the sugarpaste to about 2mm (¹/₁₆") thick, put a paper template over the paste and cut each piece of paste a little bigger than the template. Leave it lying flat overnight to harden the surface.

6 Cut the sugarpaste to fit the shape of each cookie exactly. Place the tracing paper with the pattern over the surface of the sugarpaste and trace over the lines with a bamboo skewer.

7 Fit a piping bag with a no. 0 nozzle and pipe red-coloured royal icing over the flower and leaf lines. Finish one flower with the brush embroidery technique as described earlier in this project, on page 44. Glue each part to the respective cookie with royal icing.

Valentine's Wedding Cake

(FEBRUARY)

Edibles

3 x round cakes:

25.5cm (10") x 8cm (3¹⁄₈") deep for bottom tier

23cm (9") x 8cm deep (3¹⁄₈") for middle tier

18cm (7") x 6cm (2³⁄₈") deep for top tier

2.7kg (6lb) marzipan (SK)

3.6kg (7lb 14oz) sugarpaste/rolled fondant: 2.7kg (6lb) black, 900g (2lb) white (SK)

250g (8¾oz) SK Instant Mix Royal Icing: 100g (4oz) white, 150g (5¼oz) coloured with Jet Black

Modelling paste:

300g (11oz) white = 150g (5¼oz) White Sugar Florist Paste (SFP) + 150g (5¼oz) white sugarpaste

60g (2oz) red = 30g (1oz) Poinsettia Sugar Florist Paste (SFP) + 30g (1oz) white sugarpaste

SK Professional Paste Food Colour: Jet Black, Rose

SK Designer Bridal Satin Lustre Dust Food Colour: White Satin

SK Designer Moon Beam Dust Food Colour: Ruby

SK Edible Glue

Equipment

Basic equipment (see pages 6 to 7)

18cm, 23cm, 25.5cm (7", 9", 10") round cake boards

35.5cm (14") round cake drum

Satin ribbons:

2.5cm (1") wide x 2.3m (91") long red ribbon

1.5cm (⁵⁄₈") wide x 1.97m (77½") long black ribbon

Greaseproof paper strips: 3cm (1¹⁄₈") wide x 1.5m (59") long, 4.5cm (1¾") wide x 75cm (29½") long

Bead maker: 3mm (¹⁄₈")

Garrett frill cutter with 2.5cm (1") diameter centre circle

Half-cylinder flower former: 5.3cm x 2.2cm x 27.7cm (2¼" x ¾" x 11")

Heart leaf cutters: 20mm–45mm (¾"–1½") set of 4 (Tinkertech)

Piping nozzle: no. 0

Templates (see page 194)

Decoration

Bride figurine (see pages 58 to 61)

Covering the cake drum

1 Cover the cake drum with 900g (2lb) black sugarpaste and leave to dry (see page 35). Use a non-toxic glue stick or double-sided tape to attach a length of black satin ribbon around the edge of the drum (see page 39).

2 Place a 25.5cm (10") cake board centrally on top of the drum, mark around its circumference with a scribing needle then remove the board.

Pearl hearts

3 Copy the heart templates onto a sheet of paper approximately 6cm x 25cm (2³⁄₈" x 9") in size. Place the paper over the curve of a flower former then place a piece of greaseproof paper over the heart templates and secure with a small amount of royal icing.

4 Dust White Satin dust food colour over a bead maker. Make a thin sausage of white modelling paste approximately

   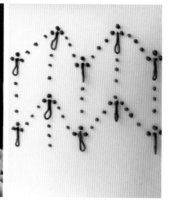

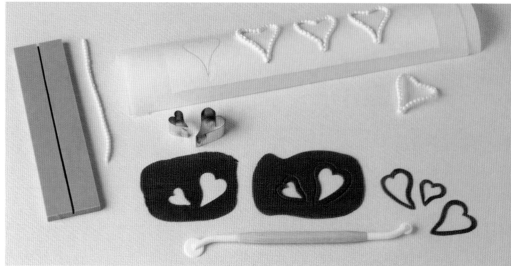

12cm (4½") long. Place this in the bead maker, press down and trim away any excess paste. Take the paste beads out of the bead maker and trim again. Cut the length of beads in half to make two 6cm (2⅜") pieces.

5 Apply edible glue to the greaseproof paper, following the outline of the heart template. Place the two lengths of beads onto the greaseproof paper to make a pearl heart and attach at the join with edible glue.

6 Repeat steps 4 and 5 to make 24 pearl hearts. When dry, remove the hearts carefully from the paper with a palette knife.

Tutor Tip

As the pearl hearts are quite fragile, it is a good idea to make several extra hearts in case of breakages.

Base tier

7 Secure the cake onto the 25.5cm (10") cake board. Cover the cake first with 1.2kg (2lb 10¼oz) of marzipan, then with 1.2kg

(2lb 10¼oz) of black sugarpaste. Let it stand for a day, then insert cake dowels to support the upper tiers (see page 38).

8 Cut the 3cm (1⅛") wide paper strip to fit around the circumference of the cake. Fold it into eight equal parts and crease the folds. Wrap the paper strip around the bottom of the cake and mark the point at the top of each crease with a scribing needle or a dress pin that has been sterilised in alcohol. Remove the tape then secure a length of red satin ribbon around the bottom of the cake.

9 Roll out some red modelling paste and cut out eight heart shapes with the second largest heart leaf cutter in the set. Discard the cut out heart shapes as you will not need them. Using a cutting wheel, cut out another heart shape about 5mm (¼") outside the heart-shaped holes in the paste and dust with Ruby iridescent dust food colour. Turn the cutter around and cut out eight more

Tutor Tip

Mix Rose paste food colour into the modelling paste until it matches the colour of the red satin ribbon.

hearts as before to make eight pairs of opposite hearts.

10 Glue each pair of hearts onto the side of the cake with the ends touching at each marked point from step 7, as shown in the picture.

11 To make the ruffles, roll out some white modelling paste, cut with a Garrett frill cutter and brush White Satin dust on both sides of the paste with a dry, flat paintbrush. Frill the edge with a bamboo skewer by pressing and rolling the skewer along the edge of the paste, then fold the paste in half and gather together, as shown in the picture. Roll the base with your fingers to extend it a little.

Tutor Tip

Make as many ruffles as you can in one sitting so that the paste does not dry out.

12 Using the circle marked on the drum earlier as a guide, place ruffles around the circumference of the circle and secure with edible glue. The base of the ruffles should sit inside the scribed line with the frilled ends outside the line so that you will see them once the bottom tier is in place. Before the ruffles dry out, secure the cake in the centre of the cake drum with royal icing.

13 Use a Garrett frill cutter to cut out more white modelling paste. Cut this ring in half, as shown, and follow step 10 to make more ruffles from this paste. Add ruffles around the base tier where necessary.

Tutor Tip

Make sure to position the ruffles so that you will still see the frilled ends when the base tier is put in place. Once the cakes are placed on top of the ruffles, the paste may be dry so make more ruffles than you need in case you have to fill in any bare patches. Remember to always bear in mind the overall appearance of the cake.

14 At this point, use dots of royal icing to secure the pearl hearts onto each pair of red hearts.

Valentine's Wedding Cake

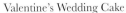

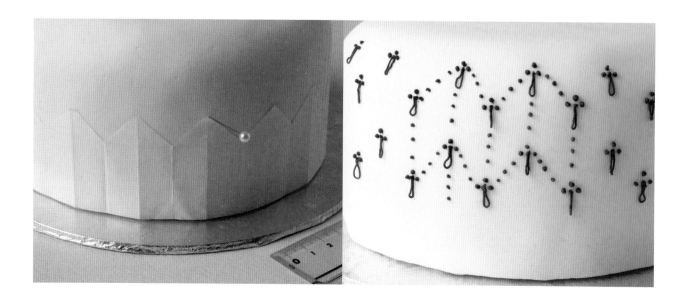

Middle tier

15 Place the 23cm (9") cake on a cake board of the same size. Cover the cake first with 900g (1lb 15¾oz) of marzipan, then with 900g (1lb 15¾oz) of white sugarpaste (see pages 30 to 34) and leave it to stand for a day.

16 Place an 18cm (7") cake board centrally on the top of the cake and mark around its circumference with a scribing needle as before. Remove the cake board and insert four cake dowels within the circle (see page 38).

17 Cut the 4.5cm (1¾") wide paper strip to fit the circumference of the cake and fold it into 24 equal parts. To do so, fold the tape in half three times and then fold it into three. Each section will be a rectangle measuring 4.5cm (1¾") x approximately 3cm (1⅛") in size. Using a ruler and pencil, mark the centre point at the top of the rectangle (the short side) then measure 1.5cm down each side from the top corners and mark with the pencil. Draw two diagonal lines up to the central

mark to make a point and cut along the lines. When you open up the paper it will look like a picket fence. Wrap the tape around the base of the cake and mark the zig-zag pattern on the cake side with a scribing needle or sterilised dress pins. Move the template up by 3cm (1⅛") and repeat to make a second set of marks directly above the first.

18 Place some black royal icing in a piping bag fitted with a no. 0 nozzle and pipe loops at the marks made in the previous step. Pipe dots to the right, left and above the loops then pipe three dots to join up each loop pattern, as shown in the picture.

19 Attach red satin ribbon around the bottom of the cake, then secure a black satin ribbon over the red one. Place the cake centrally on top of the bottom layer.

Top tier

20 Place the cake on an 18cm (7") cake board. Cover the cake first with 600g

(1lb 5¼oz) of marzipan, then with 600g (1lb 5¼oz) of black sugarpaste (see pages 30 to 34) and leave it to stand for a day.

21 Follow step 8 to mark the sides of the cake as per the bottom tier. Follow step 9 to attach the red hearts to the cake. However, for this tier use the smallest heart leaf cutter in the set for the reversed hearts.

22 Follow step 11 to make the ruffles and then glue these ruffles around the line marked earlier on the top of the cake. Place the cake on top of the middle layer, positioning the hearts between those on the bottom tier. Add extra ruffles where they are needed and attach a vertical pearl heart to each bigger red heart.

23 Fill a posy pick with black sugarpaste and insert it into the centre of the cake. Cut the wire under the foot of the bride to match the depth of the pick and insert. Fill any gap under the foot with sugarpaste. Support the bride with pieces of sugarpaste wrapped in cling film and moulded to the shape required until she is stable.

Bride

Edibles

Modelling paste:

   120g (4¼oz) white = 60g (2oz) White
   Sugar Florist Paste (SFP) + 60g (2oz)
   white sugarpaste

30g (1oz) SK Instant Mix Royal Icing: white

SK Professional Paste Food Colour:
Chestnut (soft beige)

SK Designer Pastel Dust Food Colours:
Baby Blue, Pastel Pink

SK Designer Bridal Satin Lustre Dust Food
Colour: White Satin

SK Edible Glue

White vegetable fat

Clear alcohol

Equipment

Basic equipment (see pages 6 to 8)

20-, 28- and 33-gauge floral wires: white

Piping nozzle: no. 0

CelStick (155mm x 6mm)

2cm (¾"), 3cm (1⅛"), 10.5cm (4")
round cutters

Adult head mould (small): 2.5cm (1")
long x 2cm (¾") wide (Holly Products)

15cm (6") round or square polystyrene
block, at least 10cm (4") deep (e.g. a
cake dummy)

Important note

Floral wire would not usually be used
to hold sugar models together as it is
inedible and poses a choking risk. This
model is somewhat of an exception as
the wires have been used here to bend
the bride into position. The support for the
bride must be inserted into a posy pick
and removed before the cake is served:
remember to inform the recipient that the
bride is inedible. It is worth noting that
wires should never be inserted into any
edible part of a cake or model that may be
eaten: if you need to use internal supports,
dry spaghetti and cocktail sticks are good
alternatives because they are suitable
for food contact (but again, ensure the
recipient is aware that inedible supports
have been used and must not be eaten).

Body

1 Using 10g (¼oz) of white modelling paste, shape a body that is 4cm (1½") long and 2cm (¾") wide across the shoulders, as shown in the picture. Pinch the upper part to make a neck about 1cm (³/₈") long and shape the lower part into a 'v' to make the hips. Gather the paste to make the chest and make dents in the shoulders where the arms will be attached.

2 Insert a glued 20-gauge wire that is 25.5cm (10") long into the top of the neck, through the body and down towards the right hip, leaving about 2cm (¾") protruding from the top. Insert a small piece of 28-gauge wire across the shoulders and another across the hips. Leave 5mm (¼") of wire at both ends.

Tutor Tip

Each wire should be covered with edible glue before it is inserted into the paste to hold it firmly in place. All parts of the bride will be stuck together with edible glue (see page 23).

Legs

3 Roll 12g (½oz) of white modelling paste into a 12cm (4½") long sausage that is tapered at one end. Repeat to make a second leg. Bring out the tip of the foot and heel at the tapered end of each leg and mould a small bump above the centre of the foot for the ankle. Cut the top of each leg diagonally so that it fits comfortably at the base of the hips.

4 To attach the right leg to the right side of the body, bend the long wire at the hip forward a little and insert it through the top of the thigh and down the leg so that it protrudes from the paste just below the ankle. Slightly bend the wire at the knee so that the figure stoops a little. Attach the left leg at the hip with edible glue.

5 Lay the body and legs down and leave to dry completely. Bend the wire so that the figure stays balanced and place it into a block of polystyrene to dry.

Arms

6 Take 4g (under ¼oz) of white modelling paste and make a 7cm (2¾") sausage that is tapered at one end. Hollow the tapered end to make it into a hand. Trim the paste at the inner wrist to make it thinner and to give shape to the arm. With the back of the hand facing upwards, use scissors to make a cut in the hand to bring out the thumb. Make three incisions in the rest of the hand for the fingers. Follow the same process to make the other arm.

7 When her arms are dry attach them to the body. Support them with tissue paper until both arms are fixed in place.

Head

8 To make the earrings, roll five small balls of white modelling paste and thread them onto a 33-gauge wire. Repeat to make a matching earring, dust them both with White Satin dust and leave to dry.

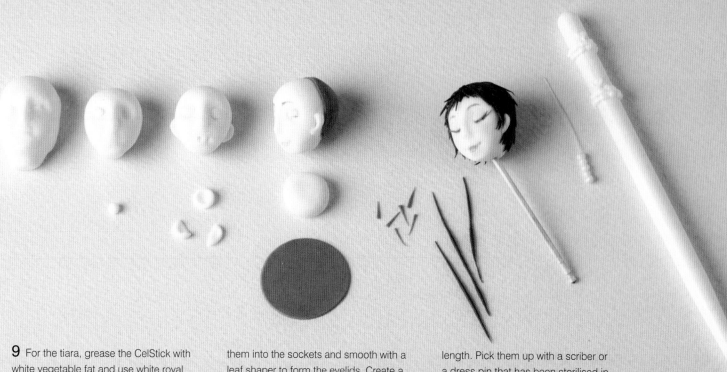

9 For the tiara, grease the CelStick with white vegetable fat and use white royal icing in a piping bag with a no. 0 piping nozzle to pipe two tiers of beads over the CelPin. Pipe a line in between the tiers and pipe a small heart at the centre. Leave to dry, then dust with White Satin dust food colour. Remove carefully from the rolling pin with the edge of a palette knife: it is a good idea to make several tiaras as they are very fragile.

10 To create the face, lightly grease the inside of the face mould with white vegetable fat using a small brush and then roll 10g (¼oz) of white modelling paste into a ball. Fill the head mould with the paste and press firmly so that it picks up the fine detail. Carefully remove the paste from the mould and reshape the face if necessary so that it is 2.5cm (1") long by 2cm (¾") wide.

11 Use a small ball tool to make two sockets for the eyes. Make two small circles with white modelling paste, place

them into the sockets and smooth with a leaf shaper to form the eyelids. Create a small hole in the centre of the face and use a cocktail stick to lift the paste on either side to make the bride's mouth.

12 For the ears, roll a ball with white modelling paste and flatten it down. Make a dent in the middle of the paste and then cut it in half to make two ears. Cut into either side of the face just below the eye line and secure the ears into the incisions.

13 To make the figure appear to be wearing make-up, dust Pastel Pink over the cheeks and the mouth, and Baby Blue dust colour on the eyelids. Mix a little Chestnut paste food colour with clear alcohol and use a fine paintbrush to paint on the bride's eyebrows.

14 For the eyelashes, colour a tiny piece of white modelling paste with Chestnut paste food colour to make it pale brown. Use your fingers to roll the paste into thin sausages approximately 5mm (¼") in

length. Pick them up with a scriber or a dress pin that has been sterilised in alcohol and carefully arrange them along the lower eyelids.

15 Roll a small piece of white modelling paste and attach it to the back of the head to make it rounded. Roll out more Chestnut modelling paste, cut a circle with a 3cm (1⅛") round cutter and glue this to the back of the head. Insert a cocktail stick into the neck and leave it to dry in a piece of polystyrene.

16 Roll a small amount of brown modelling paste with your fingers and make thin sausages that are 2mm–5mm (⅛"–¼") long for the strands of hair. At first, glue the strands sparsely over the entire head and then add more where it is needed. When the hair is nearly finished, attach the earrings just below the ears and secure the tiara. To finish, attach more strands of hair around the earrings and tiara.

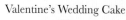

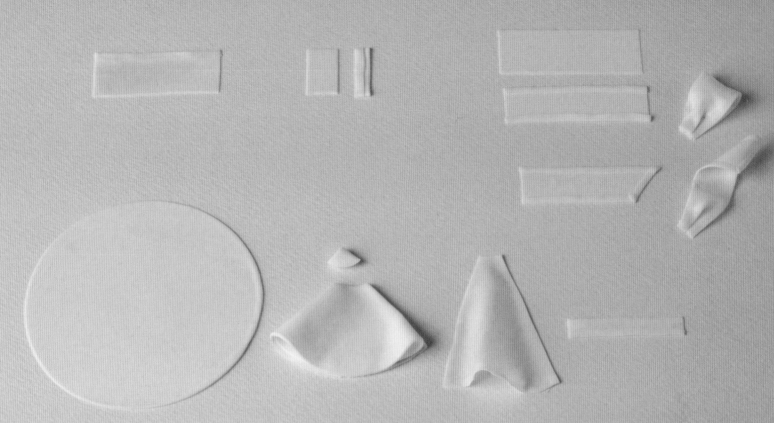

Dress

Tutor Tip

When you are making the dress, dust White Satin dust food colour over each part of the dress to make the bride shimmer. Fold back the edges of each piece of paste you cut to give the dress a neat finish.

17 Thinly roll out 30g (1oz) of white modelling paste. Cut out a rectangle measuring 6cm x 3cm (2³/₈" x 1¹/₈") and glue it around the bride's chest.

18 Cut out another piece of modelling paste with a 10cm (4") round cutter and fold it gently into four. Place the centre of a 2cm (¾") round cutter at the top of the fold and cut away the tip. Unfold the paste and divide it into eight equal parts to make an eight-panel skirt.

19 Use a rolling pin to lengthen the skirt to about 7cm (2¾") and flare out the hem with a large ball tool. Attach two pieces of the skirt to the front of the body and arrange them so that the bride's legs can still be seen, as shown in the picture. Glue the other six pieces evenly around the body, behind the first two. Make a 5cm x 1.5cm (2" x ⁵/₈") sash from white modelling paste, wrap it around her waist and secure in place.

Shoulder straps and bow

20 Thinly roll out 20g (¾oz) of white modelling paste, cut out a 2.5cm x 1.5cm (1" x ⁵/₈") rectangle and pleat along the longer side. Make another of these, glue them over the shoulders to make straps for the dress and trim away any excess.

21 Cut out another rectangle from the modelling paste measuring 14cm x 2.5cm (5½" x 1"). Cut both ends diagonally and then cut it in half. Gently bend the paste to make the edges of the two 7cm (2¾") pieces wavy.

22 Follow the same process and make three more rectangles measuring 6cm x 2.5cm (2³/₈" x 1"). Join the ends of each to make three rings. When these are semi-dry but still slightly soft, glue the two curved ribbons to the back of the dress and attach three rings above them to form a bow. Support them with tissue paper until they are secure.

23 To finish, remove the cocktail stick from the head and secure the head onto the wire coming out of the neck.

Early Spring Chic

(MARCH)

Edibles

2 x round cakes:

25.5cm (10") x 10cm (4") deep for bottom tier

15cm (6") x 7.5cm (3") deep for top tier

1.4kg (2lb 3oz) marzipan (SK)

2.65kg (3lb 1oz) sugarpaste/rolled fondant: white (SK)

Modelling paste:

600g (1lb 5¼oz) yellow = 300g (10½oz) Pale Yellow Sugar Florist Paste (SFP) + 300g (10½oz) white sugarpaste

SK Sugar Florist Paste (SFP): Cream, Pale Green, White

A small amount of SK Instant Mix Royal Icing

SK Professional Paste Food Colour: Daffodil

SK Designer Bridal Satin Lustre Dust Food Colour: White Satin

SK Edible Glue

Icing/confectioners' sugar

Equipment

Basic equipment (see pages 6 to 7)

43cm (17") round cake drum

12.5cm and 23cm (5" and 9") round cake boards

18cm (7") round cake card

12cm (5") x 10cm (4") deep round polystyrene dummy cake

Satin ribbon: 1.5cm (⁵/₈") wide x 1.4m (55") long white, 1.3cm (½") wide x 50cm (19¾") long yellow, 2.4cm (1") wide x 1.8m (71") long yellow

Round cutters: 3cm, 5cm (1¹/₈", 2")

Aluminium foil

Pointed tweezers

Decoration

15 Persian buttercups, 9 daffodils, 6 gardenia flowers, 6 gardenia buds (see pages 68 to 71)

12 mini cakes (see pages 74 to 75)

Cake drum

1 Cover the cake drum with 950g (2lb 1¼oz) of white sugarpaste as explained on page 35, and leave it to dry for several days.

Bottom tier

2 Trim off the top of the 25.5cm (10") cake with a sharp knife to give it a flat surface, then place an 18cm (7") cake card centrally on top of the cake. Insert cocktail sticks at 5cm (2") intervals around the sides of the cake, about 3cm (1¹/₈") down from the top of the cake. With a sharp knife, cut away the cake between the cake card and the cocktail sticks to make the top of the cake domed, then remove the card and sticks. Secure this domed cake to the centre of a 23cm (9") cake board, then measure 1.5cm (½") from the bottom of the cake and cut away the bottom of the cake between this and the cake board.

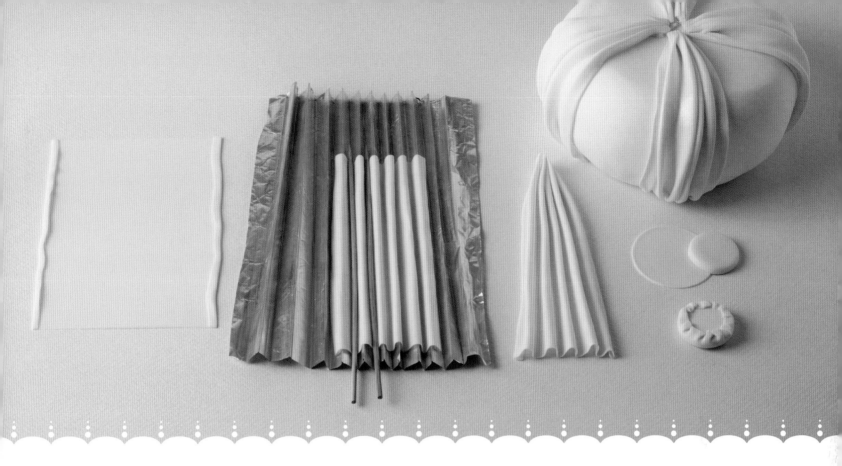

3 Cover the cake with 900g (2lb) of marzipan and 900g (2lb) of white sugarpaste (see pages 30 to 34). Use a modelling tool to make four marks on the top of the cake that are 6.5cm (2½") from the centre (see page 37, how to mark a cake, for guidance). Place a 12cm (5") cake board in the centre of the cake, following the marks as a guide, and draw around its circumference with a cocktail stick. Insert the cake dowels accordingly within the circle (see page 38).

4 Cut the aluminium foil into a rectangle measuring 22cm x 25cm (8½" x 10"). Fold the short side of the rectangle into 1.5cm (⁵/₈") wide concertina pleats.

5 Thinly roll out the modelling paste and cut out a 12cm x 18cm (5" x 7") rectangle. If you are using a pasta machine, turn the dial from 1 to 5 then cut to size. (Refer to the English Rose Cake, page 90.) Fold back the edges of the longer sides and brush White Satin dust over the upper side of the paste.

6 Dust a small amount of icing sugar over the aluminium foil. Place the rectangle of modelling paste onto the foil with the dusted side up and with the 18cm (7") side of the paste parallel to the 22cm (8½") side of the

foil. Hold a skewer in each hand and press the sugarpaste into the creases in the foil to make pleats in the paste. When you have pleated the whole piece of modelling paste, slide it off the aluminium foil and hold the top and bottom of the paste to adjust the pleats.

7 Brush edible glue at the points you marked on the cake earlier. Make pleats in the same way as before and stick them from the bottom of the cake to the top on four sides to create a cross shape. Attach pleats to the right and the left of those first pleats, then on the opposite sides. Continue the process all around the cake until it is covered.

Tutor Tip

After you have glued down one set of pleats, glue another on the opposite side: this way the pleats will line up around the cake.

Top tier

8 Trim off the top of the 15cm (6") cake with a sharp knife to give it a flat surface,

then place a 12cm (5") cake board centrally on top of the 15cm (6") cake. Insert cocktail sticks at 5cm (2") intervals around the sides of the cake, about 3cm (1¹/₈") down from the top of the cake. In the same way as for the bottom tier, cut away the cake between the cake board and the cocktail sticks, then remove them. Secure this cake to the centre of the 12.5cm (5") cake board. Measure 1.5cm (½") from the bottom of the cake and cut away the cake between this line and the cake board.

9 Cover the cake with 500g (1lb 1¾oz) marzipan and 500g (1lb 1¾oz) white sugarpaste (see pages 30 to 34).

10 Roll out some modelling paste and cut out a rectangle measuring 12cm x 16cm (5" x 6½"). Fold back the longer sides of the paste and brush with White Satin dust as before. Place the dusted modelling paste on the same concertinaed foil you used previously, with the long side of the paste parallel to the short side of the foil. Make pleats in the same way as before and stick them all around the cake, gluing each one from the bottom of the cake to the top.

11 Place a 3cm (1⅛") round cutter centrally on top of the cake, press down to cut out the sugarpaste and smooth down the cut edge with your fingers. Using the same cutter, cut out a circle of modelling paste that is about 5mm (¼") thick and again smooth the edges with your fingers.

12 Thinly roll out some more modelling paste and cut out a 5cm (2") circle. Wrap the 5mm (¼") thick piece of modelling paste around this fresh piece of paste. Dust with White Satin dust food colour and use edible glue to stick it into the hole in the surface of the cake covering.

Flower separator

Tutor Tip

If you wish to use a real cake for this flower separator instead of a polystyrene dummy, secure a 12cm (5") round cake to a cake board of the same size and cover it with 400g (14oz) of marzipan and 400g (14oz) of sugarpaste. Cover the top and the sides separately, leave it for one day and then insert the cake dowels (see page 38). If this tier is to be eaten, make the sugar flowers without wires. To attach them to the cake, make dents in the sugarpaste on the sides of the cake and secure the flowers in place with royal icing.

13 Roll out some white sugarpaste to 5mm (¼") thick and cut out two rectangles 18.5cm x 10cm (7" x 4") in size. Brush a little water over the side of the polystyrene and attach the two rectangles around the sides of the dummy. Smooth out the joins between them with a cake smoother.

14 Use royal icing to secure the dummy to the circle you made on the bottom tier in step 3. Divide the circumference of the dummy into three equal parts then use this to make three equally spaced marks halfway up the sides of the dummy. Use a ball tool to make dents in the sugarpaste at the three marks, then make holes with a bamboo skewer and apply edible glue to each mark. Pick up a buttercup at the base of the flower with pointed tweezers and insert it into the hole. Insert three or four flowers into each hole.

Tutor Tip

Use the handle of a small paintbrush to gently arrange the flowers and leaves so that they cover any gaps around the side of the cake.

15 Insert several gardenias (both flowers and buds) and daffodils in the same way as for the buttercups, with the buttercups at the centre. Completely cover the sides of the cake with white flowerets (see page 99, English Rose Cake).

16 Roll out some Cream SFP and cut out one of each size 5-petal flowers with cutter nos. 7–10. Layer the petals, starting with the largest at the bottom, and press them with the end of a fine paintbrush to cup them. Roll out some green SFP and cut out several leaves (see page 184). Use these flowers and leaves whilst they are still soft to fill any gaps in the flower separator.

Assembly

17 Once the cake drum is dry, place a 25.5cm (10") round cake stand in the centre. Place the bottom tier and the flower separator onto the stand, then secure the top tier onto the flower tier with royal icing.

18 Tape four stems of buttercups together with floral tape. Wrap a 1.3cm (½") wide yellow satin ribbon around the stems, tie into a bow and place on the top tier.

19 Make three bows with the 2.4cm (1") wide yellow satin ribbon and attach them in three places at the bottom of the flower tier with wires (for a polystyrene dummy) or royal icing (for a cake, see page 24).

20 Place the mini cakes around the cake drum, then arrange the buttercups and daffodils between the mini cakes.

Daffodils, Gardenias and Persian Buttercups

Edibles

SK Sugar Florist Paste (SFP): Pale Yellow, Pale Pink, Cream, Pale Green

SK Professional Dust Food Colours: Daffodil, Vine

SK Designer Bridal Satin Lustre Dust Food Colours: Chiffon Pink, White Satin

SK Designer Pollen Style Edible Dust Food Colour: Pale Yellow

SK Edible Glue

Equipment

Basic equipment (see page 8)

24-, 26-gauge floral wires: green

30-gauge floral wire: white

Floral tape: green (half-width)

Large carnation cutter (Orchard Products)

Rose petal cutter: 2.5cm (1") x 4cm (1½") from set of 4 (PME)

Sponge flower pad with holes

5-petal cutters: F5 5cm (2"), F6 6cm (2³/₈") (Orchard Products)

Round polystyrene formers: 2cm, 2.5cm, 3cm, 4cm (¾",1", 1¹/₈", 1½")

Set of 5 rose petal cutters (FMM):

    A 4cm x 4.5cm (1½" x 1¾")

    B 3cm x 3.5cm (1³/₈" x 1³/₈")

    C 3cm x 3cm (1¹/₈" x 1¹/₈")

    D 2cm x 2cm (¾" x ¾")

    E 1.5cm x 1.5cm (⁵/₈" x ⁵/₈")

Daffodil

Trumpet

1 Take a small amount of Pale Yellow SFP and make a teardrop shape approximately 1cm (³/₈") long. Use fine, pointed scissors to make three cuts in the top of the paste. Insert a glued 26-gauge wire into the base of the teardrop and leave to dry.

2 Make six 1.5cm (⁵/₈") long cones of Pale Green SFP, glue them around the yellow teardrop to make the flower centre and leave to dry. Once dry, brush edible glue at the top of the flower centre and dust with Pale Yellow edible pollen.

3 Form a Mexican hat shape from Pale Yellow SFP and cut out with a large carnation cutter (see page 186). Place the paste on a sponge pad and use a bone tool to stretch out the petals. To curve the petals, pull a ball tool from the top to the base of each petal then cup them with a CelPin.

4 To make the daffodil trumpet push the wire attached to the flower centre through the middle of the pale yellow petals. Dust Daffodil dust food colour across the top of the trumpet and Vine dust food colour over the base.

Petals

5 Roll out a small piece of Pale Yellow SFP, leaving a mound at the centre for a wire. Invert the 2.5cm x 4cm (1' x 1½") rose petal cutter and cut out a petal from this paste. Repeat to make five more petals. Cut the bottom edges of each petal to give them a more angular shape and insert a 30-gauge white wire into the mound of each petal.

6 Vein each petal with a bamboo skewer, smooth the petals' edges and dust the edges with Daffodil dust food colour.

Assembly

7 Before the petals are dry, position three petals so that they are equally spaced around the trumpet and tape in place. Tape three more petals around them, in-between the first petals.

Gardenia

Flower

1 Make a rugby ball shape from a small amount of Pale Yellow SFP. Attach the paste to the end of a 26-gauge wire and leave to dry. Once dry, cover the paste with edible glue and dust with Pale Yellow edible pollen.

2 Form a Mexican hat shape with some Cream SFP and cut out a flower shape using the 5cm (2") 5-petal cutter. Smooth the petal edges with a flower shaping tool and then place the flower on a foam pad. To cup and shape each petal, press the flat edge of a CelPin against the flower centre and curl each petal around the CelPin. Push the wire with the attached flower centre through the middle of the petals, secure the petals to the flower centre with edible glue and leave to dry.

3 Thinly roll out some Pale Yellow SFP and cut out two flowers using a 6cm (2³⁄₈") 5-petal cutter. Smooth the petal edges with a flower shaping tool then push them up the wire so they sit behind the flower centre. Attach one petal at a time, making sure that the petals open out gradually.

4 To make a bud, make another flower using the 6cm (2³⁄₈") 5-petal cutter, push it up the wire and glue close to the petals.

Persian Buttercup

Base

1 Insert a hooked 24-gauge wire into a 2.5cm (1") round polystyrene former.

Petals: first layer

2 Mix some Pale Yellow and Pale Green SFP, roll out thinly and cut out five petals with rose cutter E. Attach the petals to the top of the polystyrene with edible glue, overlapping each petal.

Second layer

3 Thinly roll out some Pale Pink SFP and cut out five petals with rose cutter D. Vein the petals with a veining tool, smooth the edges with a flower shaping tool and lightly dust with White Satin dust food colour. To cup, place them over a 2cm (³⁄₄") round polystyrene former and pinch along the curve of each petal. Glue them around the first row of petals, making them slightly more open.

Tutor Tip

Stick the petals closely together so that they will not open out and distort the shape of the flower.

Third to fifth layers

4 Repeat the previous steps and make the next three layers of petals. Make five petals for each layer using the following cutters and polystyrene formers. Glue five outer petals and five inner petals to the flower alternately.

- Third layer: rose cutter C, 2.5cm (1") former
- Fourth layer: rose cutter B, 3cm (1⅛") former
- Fifth layer: rose cutter A, 4cm (1½") former

Sixth layer

5 Thinly roll out some Pale Pink SFP and cut out two strips. Place a wire on one piece, and layer one on top of the other so that the wire is sandwiched between the two. Roll out the paste further around the wire and cut out a petal with rose cutter A. Repeat to make five petals. Shape the petals in the same way as before and cup them using a 4cm (1½") polystyrene former. Tape them behind the fifth row with floral tape. Dust Chiffon Pink over the edges of the petals.

6 For the cream and pink flowers, lightly combine some Cream SFP with a small amount of Pale Pink SFP. Make the flowers following the method above and

dust with Chiffon Pink dust food colour to adjust the colour to your liking.

Calyx

7 Cut the end of the floral tape into a point and pull the tape with your fingers to stretch and twist the end. Make five and tape them around the base of each flower with more floral tape.

Tutor Tip

Only attach a calyx made of floral tape to the flowers that will be used to make a bouquet as the calyces on the separator flowers won't be seen.

Mini Cakes

Edibles

12 round cakes: 5cm (2") x 5cm (2") deep

To decorate each cake:

40g (1½oz) marzipan (SK)

40g (1½oz) sugarpaste: white (SK)

40g (1½oz) modelling paste:

   20g (¾oz) pink = 10g (¼oz) Pale Pink Sugar Florist Paste (SFP) + 10g (¼oz) white sugarpaste

   20g (¾oz) yellow = 10g (¼oz) Pale Yellow Sugar Florist Paste (SFP) + 10g (¼oz) white sugarpaste

SK Sugar Florist Paste (SFP): Pale Green, Pale Pink, Pale Yellow

SK Professional Dust Food Colours: Rose, Vine

SK Designer Bridal Satin Lustre Dust Food Colours: Chiffon Pink, White Satin

SK Designer Pollen Style Edible Dust Colour: Pale Yellow

SK Edible Glue

Icing/confectioners' sugar

Equipment

Basic equipment (see pages 6 to 7)

2.2cm (¾"), 2.5cm (1") round cutters

Daisy cutter, no. 4: 4.5cm (1¾") (FMM)

Calyx cutter, R11: 43mm (1½") from Rose Calyx & Briar Rose Cutter set (Orchard Products)

Cupped former (e.g. apple tray)

Cake

1 Cover the cake with 40g (1½oz) of marzipan, then with 40g (1½oz) of sugarpaste (see pages 30 to 34).

2 Thinly roll out some pink or yellow modelling paste and make a rectangle that is 6cm x 8cm (2⅜" x 3⅛") in size. Fold back the longer sides a little and dust White Satin dust food colour over the top of the paste.

3 Place the piece of paste on a board and sprinkle icing sugar over two bamboo skewers. Take one skewer in each hand, place one horizontally across the longer side of the paste and pull the sugarpaste with the other skewer to make pleats. Remove the skewers and shape the pleats with your fingers. Use

edible glue to stick the pleated paste from the top of each cake and down the sides. Make three more pleated bands of paste and stick them around the cake, as shown in the picture.

4 Use a ball tool to make a dent in the top of each cake and use edible glue or royal icing to secure daisies to the cakes with yellow pleats and buttercups to the cakes with pink pleats.

Flowerets

Daisy

1 Roll out some Pale Yellow SFP and cut out two sets of petals with a daisy cutter. Glue one set of petals on top of the other with one set of petals between the other. Place them over a curved former (such as an apple tray) and leave to dry.

2 Make a small ball of Pale Yellow SFP and flatten the surface a little. Brush a small amount of edible glue over the top of the ball, dust with Pale Yellow pollen and attach the ball to the centre of the petals with a cocktail stick.

3 Roll out some Pale Green SFP and cut out a calyx. Stretch out the edges with a bone tool and glue at the base of the daisy.

Buttercup

1 Make a ball with 2g (under ¼oz) of Pale Green SFP, flatten it a little and leave to dry.

2 Thinly roll out some Pale Pink SFP, cut out three petals with a 2.2cm (¾") round cutter and five petals with a 2.5cm (1") round cutter.

3 Fold each petal in half and place the centre of the fold at the same point in the centre of the SFP ball. Glue the three 2.2cm (¾") petals evenly to cover the rest of the ball. In the same way fold five 2.5cm (1") petals and glue evenly around the ball.

4 Make and attach a calyx in the same way as for the daisy and brush Chiffon Pink and Rose dusts around the petal edges.

Flower Festival Cake

(APRIL)

Edibles

4 x hexagonal cakes:

  18cm (7") x 10cm (4") deep for bottom tier

  15cm (6") x 5cm (2") deep for first tier

  13cm (5") x 7cm (2¾") deep for second tier

  10cm (4") x 10cm (4") deep for top tier

2.2kg (4lb 13oz) marzipan (SK)

2.2kg (4lb 13oz) sugarpaste/rolled fondant: 300g (10½oz) white, 1.5kg (3lb 5oz) pink, 400g (14oz) green (SK)

200g (7oz) SK Instant Mix Royal Icing

300g (10½oz) SK Instant Mix Run-Out Icing

SK Professional Paste Food Colours: Chestnut, Poinsettia, Vine

SK Professional Liquid Food Colours: Chestnut, Rose

SK Designer Metallic Lustre Dust Food Colour: Gold

SK Designer Bridal Satin Lustre Dust Food Colour: White Satin

SK Edible Glue

Clear alcohol

Equipment

Basic equipment (see pages 6 to 7)

18cm, 15cm, 13cm and 10cm (7", 6", 5" and 4") hexagonal cake boards

Piping nozzles: nos. 0, 1

Long-bladed sharp scissors

Tracing paper

Templates (see page 195)

Decoration

Kanzashi (Japanese ornamental hairpin)

Preparation

1 Use a few drops of Chestnut liquid food colour to make the royal icing pale brown and a few drops of Rose liquid food colour to make the run-out icing pink.

Bottom tier

2 Secure the 18cm (7") cake onto a cake board of the same size and weigh out 800g (1lb 12oz) marzipan. Cover the top of the cake with marzipan and cut neatly around the edges. With the leftover marzipan make two bands that are 10cm (4") wide and 33cm (13") long then glue these around the sides of the cake.

3 Cover the top of the cake with 340g (12oz) of pink sugarpaste. Mix another 340g (12oz) pink sugarpaste and 120g (4½oz) white sugarpaste to achieve a marbled effect. Roll out the marbled paste so that it is 2mm (1/16") thick and cut into a rectangle that is 11cm x 12cm (4½" x 5") in size. Make six of these panels and

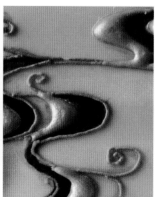

them to dry for one day. Dust the white sections of the sugarpaste panels with White Satin lustre dust and then follow the steps below to decorate and attach the panels.

4 Trace the pattern from the template onto the sugarpaste panels using a skewer or cocktail stick (as for the Camellia Cake, page 44).

5 Dilute Chestnut and Poinsettia paste food colours together in a small amount of alcohol and use a fine paintbrush to paint over the pattern. Paint the colours 3–5mm (^{1}/$_8$"–^{1}/$_4$") in from the edge of the petals.

6 Fit a piping bag with a no. 0 nozzle, fill with pale brown royal icing and use this to pipe over the outline of the pattern. Use a fine paintbrush and Gold lustre dust dissolved in clear alcohol to paint over the piped line once it has dried.

7 Place some white run-out icing in a piping bag fitted with a no. 1 nozzle and flood the petals in the pattern. (For further information on run-out icing, see page 25 and 28.) When the icing has dried, dust the white petals with White Satin lustre dust food colour. Brush Vine dust food colour over the flower centre, as shown in the picture.

8 Using a no. 0 nozzle, pipe over the flower centre with white royal icing and paint with Gold lustre dust mixed with clear alcohol when dry.

9 Line up the finished panels with the sides of the cake. Remove any excess paste with scissors and trim the base of the panels to ensure they are all the same height. Brush each side of the cake with a thin layer of royal icing and attach the panels to the sides of the cake.

First tier

10 Secure the 15cm (6") cake onto a cake board of the same size and weigh out 500g (8¾oz) marzipan. Cover the top of the cake and trim to size. With the leftover marzipan, make two bands that are 5.5cm (2¼") wide and 28cm (11") long and stick these around the sides of the cake.

11 Cover the top of the cake with 200g (7oz) green sugarpaste. Divide another 200g (7oz) green sugarpaste into three then do the same with 100g (3½oz) white sugarpaste. Use one third of the green paste and one third of the white paste to make two panels.

12 Make two sausages from one third of the green sugarpaste and do the same with the white sugarpaste. Stack the

Tutor Tip

I recommend using scissors with blades long enough to cut down the side of the paste in one go. For a clean cut, cut the panels into shape before they are too dry.

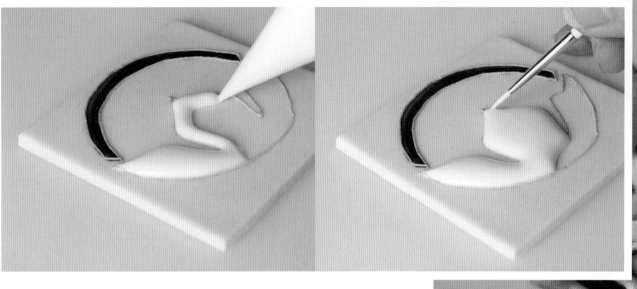

colours alternately and twist them until the paste makes horizontal stripes. Roll the paste out sideways until it is 2mm ($^1/_{16}$") thick and cut the paste into a rectangle that is 20cm x 5.5cm (8" x 2¼") in size. Cut the paste in half and repeat these steps three times to make six rectangles. Leave them to dry for a day.

13 Follow steps 4 to 7 for making sugarpaste panels, using the pattern in the picture as a guide. Paint along the curve of the wave pattern and flood the pattern with pink run-out icing. Once you have completed these steps, skip step 8 and go straight to step 9.

Second tier

14 Secure the 13cm (5") cake onto a cake board of the same size and weigh out 500g (1lb 1¾oz) marzipan. Cover the top of the cake and cut to size. With the leftover marzipan make two bands that are 7.5cm (3") wide and 24cm (9½") long and stick these around the sides of the cake as before.

15 Cover the top of the cake with 250g (8¾oz) pink sugarpaste. Roll out another 250g (8¾oz) of pink sugarpaste to 2mm ($^1/_{16}$") thick and cut into a rectangle measuring 8cm x 8.5cm (3$^1/_8$" x 3$^3/_8$"). Make six of these rectangular panels and leave them to dry for a day.

16 Follow steps 4 to 9 for making sugarpaste panels, using the pattern in the picture as a guide. However, when you get to step 5 paint inside the semicircle band.

Top tier

17 Secure the 10cm (4") cake onto a board of the same size and weigh out 400g (14oz) marzipan. Cover the top of the cake as before. Using the leftover marzipan make two rectangles that are 10cm x 20.5cm (4" x 8") in size. Stick these around the sides of the cake.

18 Cover the top of the cake with 160g (5½oz) of pink sugarpaste. Mix 160g (5½oz) of pink sugarpaste with 80g (2¾oz) white sugarpaste to make a marbled pattern. Roll out the marbled paste until it is 2mm ($^1/_{16}$") thick and cut into six 11cm x 7.5cm (4¼" x 3") rectangles. Leave them to dry for a day

then brush White Satin lustre dust over the white sections of the sugarpaste.

19 Follow steps 4 to 9 for making sugarpaste panels, using the template as a guide. However, when you get to step 5 paint leaf patterns with Chestnut and Vine paste food colours dissolved in alcohol.

20 When the top of the sugarpaste is dry, trace petals onto it. Paint stalks and leaves with Vine paste food colour to match the pattern on the sides of the top tier, then follow steps 6 to 8.

Assembly

21 Insert cake dowels into all the cakes, excluding the top tier (see page 38). Place the bottom tier onto a cake stand then stack the first, second and top tiers and secure each one in place with royal icing.

22 Make a ball of sugarpaste and place it on the cake stand at the foot of the cake. Attach the Kanzashi to this paste to finish the design.

Tutor Tips

As sugarpaste can easily change shape as you work with it, it is a good idea to cut out each panel so that it is slightly larger than the size you need and then cut the panel to the exact size just before you attach it to the cake. You should also use thin, run-out icing to attach the panels to the cake as this will give the cake a neater finish.

Kanzashi

(JAPANESE ORNAMENTAL HAIRPIN)

Edibles

SK Sugar Florist Paste (SFP): Pale Green, Pale Pink, Poinsettia, Soft Lilac, White

SK Designer Bridal Satin Lustre Dust Food Colours: Damask Rose, White Satin

SK Designer Metallic Lustre Dust Food Colour: Gold Sparkles

SK Edible Glue

Equipment

26-, 30-, 32-gauge floral wires: white

Floral tape: white (half-width and full-width)

3mm (1/8") strip cutter

Piping nozzle: no. 0

Preparation

1 Mix together Pale Pink and Poinsettia SFP to make deep pink flower paste. Mix together Pale Pink and White SFP to make pale pink flower paste.

Flower

2 Make a small ball of White SFP. Cover a hooked 30-gauge wire with edible glue, insert it into the ball and leave to dry. Dust with White Satin lustre dust.

3 Thinly roll out some of the dark pink SFP and cut out four 2.5cm (1") squares. Fold one of the squares in half to make a triangle. With the long side of the triangle at the top, place a glued, hooked wire in the centre and fold the paste over it. Fold back the corners of the paste, then cut them parallel to the wire.

4 Repeat steps 2 and 3 to make four wired petals then dust them all with Damask Rose lustre dust and leave to dry. Using half-width white floral tape, attach the four wired petals around the white flower centre.

5 Thinly roll out some pale pink SFP and cut out eight 3cm (11/8") squares. Repeat steps 2 and 3 to make eight pale pink wired petals. Dust each of the petals with White Satin lustre dust and leave to dry. Using half-width white floral tape, tape the eight pale pink wired petals around the first set of petals.

Leaves

6 Thinly roll out Pale Green SFP and cut out two 2.5cm (1") squares and one 3cm (11/8") square.

7 Using the green SFP, follow steps 2 and 3 for making petals and then leave to dry. Use white half-width floral tape to attach the two smaller leaves either side of the larger leaf.

Bouquet

8 Choose one flower to be the centre of the bouquet. Using full-width white floral tape, tape five flowers around this central flower. Tape five leaves behind the flowers.

Ornamental pin

9 Make a small rugby ball shape from Soft Lilac SFP then insert a glued 26-gauge wire into the paste. Place it onto a board and use your fingers to roll the purple paste along the wire, making a thin sausage approximately 5cm (2") long.

10 Make a small ball from Soft Lilac SFP, attach it to the end of the wire to make the head of the pin and leave to dry.

11 Repeat steps 9 and 10 using Poinsettia SFP to make a red pin. Dust all the pins with Gold Sparkles dust food colour.

'Gin bira' ribbons

12 Thinly roll out some White SFP and use a 3mm (1/8") strip cutter to make 5cm (1") long strips. Dust with White Satin lustre dust food colour and then use a no. 0 piping nozzle to make a small hole at one end of each of the strips. Make approximately 15–20 strips of paste. Cut a small piece of 32-gauge wire, insert it through the hole in the paste, twist the wire to make a ring and repeat for every strip.

13 Line up the strips in a row and insert a white 26-gauge wire through all the rings. Twist to secure and leave the remaining wire.

Assembly

14 Make two flower bouquets and tape several ornamental pins around them with white floral tape. Hang the ribbons at the foot of the bouquet and tape to secure.

Flower Festival Cookies

For my recommended cookie recipe and tips on how to ice cookies, see pages 16 and 28.

Kimono girl

I made the kimono girl in the picture as a decorative presentation piece. She is made of modelling paste and her hair has been piped with black royal icing and a very fine no. 00 nozzle.

Temari balls

These decorative Temari cake balls have been covered with black sugarpaste and the lines have been piped using a no. 00 nozzle with red, blue and yellow royal icing. See page 172 for steps on how to cover a ball with sugarpaste.

Sakura (cherry blossom) petals

Thinly roll out some Pale Pink SFP and cut out a petal with a small rose cutter. Cut a 'v' shape into the tip of the petal using the pointed end of the cutter. Dust them with SK Professional Rose Dust Food Colour to finish.

Butterfly

Roll out some Pale Yellow SFP and cut out a small pair of butterfly wings. Vein them with a wing veiner and dust with SK Designer Light Gold Metallic Lustre Dust Food Colour. Model a small body shape out of the paste and dust with the Light Gold lustre dust. Attach each wing to the sides of the body with edible glue and support them with small balls of kitchen paper until they are secure.

Sakura (cherry blossom) cookies

To make these matching cookies, use the templates to decorate them in the same way as the sugarpaste panels for the main Flower Festival Cake. These make perfect wedding favours for guests.

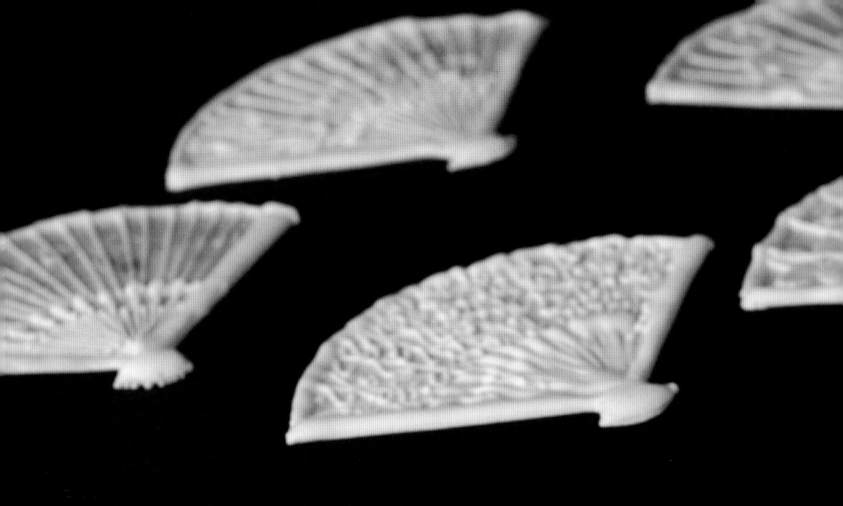

Fan cookies

Cut out each cookie (see cookie recipe on page 16) with a
Japanese fan cookie cutter (Lindy Smith). Pipe a line of stiff-peak
royal icing around the edge of the fan cookie and leave to dry.
Flood the cookies with green or pink run-out icing and once they
are dry, use green, pink and purple royal icing and a no. 0 nozzle
to pipe patterns over the cookie. To finish, use green royal icing
and a no. 0 nozzle to pipe the frame lines of the fan. See page 28
for how to create successful run-out work.

English Rose Cake

(MAY)

Edibles

4 x round cakes:

30.5cm (12") x 12cm (5") deep for
bottom tier

23cm (9") x 8cm (3") deep for second tier

18cm (7") x 15cm (6") deep for third tier

15cm (6") x 10cm (4") deep or a dummy
cake for top tier

4.2kg (9lb 4¼oz) marzipan (SK)

5.5kg (12lb 2oz) sugarpaste/rolled fondant:
4.2kg (9lb 4¼oz) pale pink, 1.3kg (2lb
13¾oz) deep pink and pale pink mixed (SK)

Small amount of SK Instant Mix Royal Icing

Modelling paste:

100g (3½oz) deep pink = 60g (2oz) Pale
Pink SFP + 40g (1½oz) white sugarpaste
+ touch of Rose paste food colour

100g (3½oz) pale pink = 60g (2oz) Pale
Pink SFP + 40g (1½oz) white sugarpaste

100g (3½oz) purple = 60g (2oz) Soft Lilac
SFP + 40g (1½oz) white sugarpaste

SK Sugar Florist Paste (SFP): Pale Pink, Soft
Lilac, White

SK Professional Paste Food Colour: Rose

SK Edible Glue

Equipment

Basic equipment (see pages 6 to 7)

15cm, 18cm, 23cm, 30cm (6", 7", 9",
12") round cake boards

48cm (19") round cake drum

Satin ribbon: 1.2cm (³⁄₈") wide x 2.9m
(114") long pink (for cakes), 1.2cm (³⁄₈")
wide x 1.55m (61") long pink (for cake
drum)

Rose leaf cutters: 2.5cm x 4cm (1" x
1½"), 2.3cm x 3cm (¾" x 1¹⁄₈") (PME)

3 posy picks

Decoration

English rose, Star-of-Bethlehem, spider
plant and floweret arrangement (see
pages 94 to 99)

Cake drum

1 Mix 1.3kg (2lb 13¾oz) of white
sugarpaste with Rose paste food colour to
make it pale pink. Add more Rose paste
food colour to a quarter of the paste to
make it a deeper shade of pink. Knead the
deep pink paste into the lighter sugarpaste
to achieve a marbled pattern and then
cover the cake drum with this marbled
paste (see page 35). Leave it to dry for
several days then attach a pink satin ribbon
around the edge with a non-toxic glue stick
or double-sided tape.

Covering the cakes

2 Mix 4.2kg (9lb 4¼oz) of white
sugarpaste with Rose paste food colour to
make it pale pink. Secure each cake onto
the cake board of the same size.

3 Cover each cake with marzipan
and then with sugarpaste. For both the
marzipan and sugarpaste, use 2kg (4lb
6½oz) for the bottom tier, 900g (2lb) for

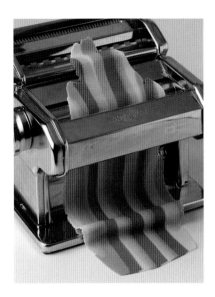
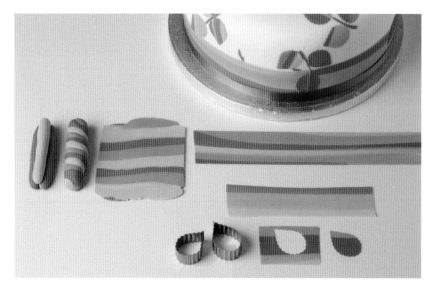

the second tier, 800g (1lb 12oz) for the third tier and 500g (1lb ¾oz) for the top tier. Insert cake dowels into all the cakes, excluding the top tier (see page 38).

Preparing the modelling paste

4 To make the modelling paste, mix SFP and sugarpaste as follows:

For the pink modelling paste, mix together 120g (4½oz) of Pale Pink SFP and 80g (2¾oz) of white sugarpaste. Colour half of this paste with Rose paste food colour and mix well to achieve deep pink modelling paste.

Tutor Tips

30g (1oz) of modelling paste will yield a strip that is 40cm (16") long and 8cm (3⅛") wide.

To work out how long a strip needs to be, measure from the base of the cake up to where it will be covered by the top tier.

For the purple modelling paste, mix 60g (2oz) Soft Lilac SFP and 40g (1½oz) white sugarpaste and knead well.

Bottom tier

5 Roll 10g (¼oz) each of deep pink, pale pink, and purple modelling paste to make three 7cm–8cm (2¾"–3⅛") long sausages. Place one sausage on top of the other two so that they are arranged in a pyramid. Hold the sausages together at either end and twist to make tricolour vertical stripes. Roll the paste out in the same direction as the stripes until the paste is 8cm (3⅛") wide and 2mm–3mm (1/16"–⅛") thick, then cut one end straight.

6 Adjust the pasta machine so that it is on the first setting and feed the paste through, cut end first. Change the settings from 2–9 and repeat the process to make thinner and longer striped bands of paste. If you don't have a pasta machine, roll the paste as thinly as possible into a long strip. Cut out eight 20cm (8") long, 4cm (1½") wide rectangles from the striped paste. From the remaining paste, cut out some leaves with a rose leaf cutter as well

as some stems and a few small pieces of paste for extra decoration.

7 Glue all the strips next to each other, from the bottom to the top of the cake from the left-hand side: the width of the strips side by side should be 28.5cm (11¼"), each overlapping by approximately 5mm (¼"). Make three more strips and, starting from the base on the right-hand side, glue them from the bottom to the top of the cake: the width of the strips side by side should be approximately 11cm (4¼"). Glue five strips at the back of the cake in the same way: they will be about 18cm (7") wide altogether.

Tutor Tip

Glue several strips from the bottom of the cake to the top, overlapping by approximately 5mm (¼") each until you achieve the desired width.

8 Glue the leaves, stems, and small pieces of paste over the cake, considering the balance of the cake as a whole. Glue some of them in groups with a large leaf at

the end of a stem and two smaller leaves either side of the stem. Once you have finished, attach a pink satin ribbon around the base of the cake then secure the cake in the centre of the cake drum.

First tier

9 Repeat steps 5 and 6 for decorating the bottom tier. However, for this tier cut out two strips that are both 38cm (15") long, place them around the bottom of the cake and glue them down at the back so the join is hidden. Glue leaves, stems and small pieces over the cake as before, then secure the cake centrally on top of the bottom tier with royal icing.

Second tier

10 Again, repeat steps 5, 6 and 7 for decorating the bottom tier. However, for this tier cut out six strips that are 25cm (10") long and 4cm (1½") wide. This time glue the strips from the top to the bottom of the cake so they are slightly slanted across the cake, as shown in the main picture. The width of all the six strips

together should be about 21.5cm (8½"). Glue leaves, stems, and small pieces of paste all over the cake. Secure the cake onto the middle of the first tier with royal icing.

Top tier

11 Repeat steps 5 and 6 for decorating the bottom tier. However, for this top tier cut out two strips that are 25.5cm (10") long and 4cm (1½") wide, then glue them around the bottom of the cake and glue leaves, stems and small pieces of paste over the cake.

12 Insert three posy picks towards the back of the cake. Tape a rose, a stem and some flowerets together with floral tape, pinch them together with a 'U'-shaped piece of wire and secure into a pick. Secure two Star-of-Bethlehem flowers into a pick on either side then attach a rose and a Star-of-Bethlehem into the pick at the back. Secure the cake centrally on top of the second tier. Place the spider plants into another a pick and attach them to the cake, making sure the cake as a finished piece looks balanced.

To finish

13 Tape two roses and some leaves together, then tape four Star-of-Bethlehem flowers together. Make a small ball of sugarpaste and place it on the cake drum a little to the left of the front of the cake. Attach the bunch of Star-of-Bethlehem flowers to the ball of paste, so they are slightly angled to the right. Attach the bouquet of roses at the foot of the bunch of Star-of-Bethlehem flowers, then attach one Star-of-Bethlehem to the left of the roses. Fill the gap between the roses and the Star-of-Bethlehem flowers with flowerets.

English Rose

Edibles

150g (5¼oz) sugarpaste/rolled fondant: pink (SK)

SK Sugar Florist Paste (SFP): Holly/Ivy, Pale Pink

SK Professional Paste Food Colour: Rose

SK Professional Dust Food Colours: Cyclamen, Holly/Ivy, Poinsettia, Rose

SK Designer Edible Pollen Dust Food Colour: Russet

SK Edible Glue

Equipment

Basic equipment (see page 8)

4cm, 5cm, 6cm (1½", 2", 2⅜") polystyrene balls

Cotton thread: yellow

20-, 30-gauge floral wires: green

30-gauge floral wires: white

Floral tape: green (full-width and half-width)

Small, medium and large carnation cutters (Orchard Products)

Rose petal cutters:

4cm x 4.5cm (1½" x 1¾") (FMM)

5.5cm x 7cm, 5cm x 5.8cm (2¼" x 2¾", 2" x 2⅜") from set of 3 (Sunflower Sugar Art)

Rose leaf cutters: 2.5cm x 5cm (1" x 2¼") large, 2.5cm x 3cm (1" x 1⅛") small (FMM)

4cm (1½") round cutter

Sandpaper

Preparation

1 Colour the sugarpaste pink with Rose paste food colour: you will need 25g (just over ¾oz) of paste for each rose. For the rose base, cut a 4cm (1½") round polystyrene ball in half and cut off the tip of the dome, then file the edges with sandpaper. Two roses can be made from one polystyrene ball.

Flower centre

2 Wind yellow cotton thread about 30 times around your index and middle fingers. Cut the thread from the reel and remove from your fingers. Twist the loop of thread in the middle to make a figure of 8 and fold over to make a smaller loop.

3 Feed a green 30-gauge wire through the loop, fold the wire in half over the cotton then twist the wire twice to fix it in place. Wind one end of the wire around the base of the loop, then twist the two wires together to make them into one. Cut the loop of thread in half, dip the ends of the thread into edible glue and cover with Russet pollen dust food colour. Tape this to a hooked green 20-gauge floral wire to make a stem.

4 Take a rose base, put it flat side down and cover it with pink sugarpaste. Use a 4cm (1½") round cutter to cut a circle of sugarpaste and glue this to the flat bottom of the base. Turn the base so the flat side is facing up; the petals will be arranged on this flat surface. Make a hole in the middle of the polystyrene with a bamboo skewer, making sure the skewer goes all the way through the ball, then fill the hole at the bottom with sugarpaste. Insert the wire stem into the hole, up to the base of the thread and leave it to dry until the wire is fixed in place. Make a sausage with a small amount of pink sugarpaste and wrap it around the bottom of the thread.

Petals

5 Thinly roll out some Pale Pink SFP and cut out two sets of petals with a small carnation cutter. Stretch each of the petal edges with a bone tool and cut each flower into quarters. Mix a little Poinsettia and Cyclamen dust with the Rose dust food colour to make a dusky pink. Dust each petal with the pink dust colour then glue them around the flower centre.

6 Roll out some more Pale Pink SFP and cut out two sets of petals with a medium-size carnation cutter and one with a large cutter, repeat step 5 and then glue them around the outside of the smaller petals. Make a sausage from the pink sugarpaste,

wrap it around the base of the petals and then smooth out the petals with your fingers.

7 Thinly roll out some Pale Pink SFP and cut out a flower with a large carnation cutter. Repeat step 5 and then glue these petals to the sugarpaste at the base of the flower.

8 Roll out some more Pale Pink SFP and cut out five petals with a 4cm x 4.5cm (1½" x 1¾") rose cutter. Vein the petals with a veining tool and curve the edges with a bone tool. Pinch the edge and place them over the top of a 5cm (2") polystyrene ball to cup them, then dust and glue around the other petals. Repeat this process using 5cm x 5.8cm (2" x 2⅜") and 5.5cm x 7cm (2¼" x 2¾") rose petal cutters and glue around the last set of petals.

9 Roll out some Pale Pink SFP and insert a white 30-gauge wire into the middle of the paste. Roll out the SFP further around the wire and cut out a 5.5cm x 7cm (2¼" x 2¾") rose petal. Repeat this step to make four more petals. Shape in the same manner as before, i.e. pinch and cup to fit the surface of a 6cm (2⅜") polystyrene

ball. Tape each petal around the last set of petals with floral tape.

Calyx

10 Cut five 8cm (3¹/₈") long pieces of full-width floral tape. Cut one end of each piece into a point and use your fingers to stretch out the tape. Cut slits down the tape as shown in the picture, dust with Holly/Ivy dust food colour and glue to each petal with edible glue. Bring together the other ends of each calyx with floral tape and wrap another piece of tape around the wire to secure them in place.

Leaves

11 Thinly roll out some Holly/Ivy SFP, leaving small mounds for each of the wires. Cut out two leaves with a large rose leaf cutter and two with a small cutter. Insert a green 30-gauge wire into each leaf and leave to dry. Tape two smaller leaves on either side and slightly below the large leaf then dust with Holly/Ivy dust food colour. Make several of these leaf sprays for the arrangement (see page 91).

Star-of-Bethlehem

Edibles

SK Sugar Florist Paste (SFP): Pale Green, White

SK Professional Paste Food Colours: Daffodil, Vine

SK Designer Pollen Style Edible Dust Food Colour: Pale Yellow

Equipment

Basic equipment (see page 8)

2.5cm (1") 6-petal cutter: no. 5 (Orchard Products)

24-gauge floral wire: green

30-gauge floral wire: white

Floral tape: green

Small round matt head stamens: white

Tutor Tip

The flower will look more natural if the teardrops and petals are not uniform in size. The size of each six-petal flower can be adjusted by varying the thickness of the paste.

1 Make a 6cm (2³/₈") long, thin teardrop shape from Pale Green SFP. Insert a green hooked 24-gauge wire into the base of the paste. Use fine pointed scissors to make alternate cuts down the paste, from the top of the teardrop to the base. Working from the base to about a third of the height, splay the cut paste with a CelPin. Use very small amounts of White SFP to make tiny teardrops and sandwich them between the incisions. Slightly bend the tip of the teardrop paste and leave to dry.

2 Roll some more small White SFP teardrops, insert a hooked white 30-gauge wire into each and leave to dry. Roll out some Pale Green SFP, cut into the white teardrops and glue them onto the side of the white teardrops. Make several of these.

3 Make a small rugby ball shape from the Pale Green SFP, insert a white 30-gauge hooked wire into the paste and leave to dry. Use floral tape to tape six small yellow stamens to this rugby ball shape, then brush edible glue onto the edges of the stamens and at the flower's centre and dust with yellow pollen.

4 Use some more White SFP to create small Mexican hat shapes (see page 186) and cut with a 6-petal cutter. Use a CelPin to cup and raise each of the petals and use your fingers to arrange them into three inner petals and three outer petals. Dust the flower centre with Daffodil dust food colour, insert the taped stamens into the centre and leave to dry. Make several of these.

5 Use floral tape to attach the teardrops one by one at the foot of the shoot, starting with the smaller ones first. Use floral tape to attach the flowers below the teardrops, again starting with the smaller ones first. Dust with Vine dust food colour to make it look more realistic.

Spider Plant

Edibles

SK Professional Sugar Florist Paste (SFP): Pale Green

SK Professional Paste Food Colour: Holly/Ivy

Equipment

Basic equipment (see page 8)

Floral tape: pale green (half-width)

28-, 30-gauge floral wires: white

22-gauge floral wires: green

10cm (4") sunflower cutter (Tinkertech)

4.5cm (1¾") daisy cutter (Tinkertech)

2cm (¾") 6-petal cutter: no. 6 (Orchard Products)

1 Make several Mexican hat shapes with some Pale Green SFP (see page 186) and cut out with a daisy cutter. Extend each petal with a bone tool and score the central line with a leaf shaper. Press the edge of a CelPin in the centre to raise the leaf and cup it. Insert a hooked white 28-gauge wire through the top. Use a fine paintbrush to paint the middle of each leaf with Holly/Ivy paste food colour to make the leaves two-toned and leave to dry.

Tutor Tip

Using a sunflower or daisy cutter allows you to make several leaves at once.

2 Roll out some more Pale Green SFP so that it is slightly thicker than usual and cut with a sunflower cutter. Separate each petal with a cutting wheel to make them into leaves. Insert a white 30-gauge wire into each leaf, roll out the paste on either side of the wire further and cut into a thin

leaf shape. Mark the central line and paint with Holly/Ivy colour in the same way as the previous leaves. Re-curve the edge of one leaf outward and tape to the leaves you made in step 1. Make about five of these leaves and tape them around the first leaves before they dry. Repeat to make several bunches in the same manner.

3 Follow the same process to make several leaves using a no. 6 six-petal cutter. Tape a green 22-gauge wire to the end of the bunches and bring together with floral tape. Add the smaller leaves to make the spider plant trail as long as you wish and tape together with floral tape.

Tutor Tip

Ensure that the colouring and positioning of each petal is not too uniform otherwise the leaves will not look natural.

Flowerets

Edibles

SK Professional Sugar Florist Paste
(SFP): Soft Lilac

SK Professional Dust Food Colour:
Violet

Equipment

Basic equipment (see page 8)

30-gauge floral wire: green

Tapered cone star modelling tool:
no. 5 (PME)

1 Make a small teardrop shape from
Soft Lilac SFP, pierce with the end of a
CelPin and press with a no. 5 star tool.
Make cuts at the marks, open them up
and leave the piece of paste face down
on the work surface.

2 Extend the five pieces of paste
with a bone tool to make them petal-
shaped. Turn the flower face up and
insert a green 30-gauge hooked and
glued wire in through the base of
the flower and secure. Tape several
flowerets together and dust the centres
with Violet dust food colour.

Hydrangea Heaven

(JUNE)

Edibles

Approximately 36 mini cakes with ribbon for stand, plus extra mini cakes without ribbon to serve, if required (see page 108)

1.25kg (2lb 12oz) SK Instant Mix Royal Icing: 250g (8¾oz) white, 250g (8¾oz) coloured with Violet, 250g (8¾oz) coloured with Rose, 250g (8¾oz) coloured with Hydrangea, 250g (8¾oz) coloured with a touch of Daffodil, 700g (1lb ⅔oz) coloured with Holly/Ivy

200g (7oz) sugarpaste/rolled fondant: green (SK)

SK Sugar Florist Paste (SFP): Holly/Ivy

SK Professional Liquid Food Colours: Daffodil, Holly/Ivy, Hydrangea, Rose, Vine, Violet

SK Professional Dust Food Colours: Holly/Ivy, Hydrangea, Rose, Vine, Violet

Equipment

Basic equipment (see pages 6 to 7)

Polystyrene cone: 5cm (2") diameter base x 7cm (2¾") diameter top x 6cm (2⅜") height

Polystyrene hemispheres: 3 x 6cm, 2 x 5cm (2⅜", 2")

Polystyrene balls: 4 x 3cm (1⅛")

Piping nozzles: nos. 1, 2, 3, 5, 10, 14, 16, 67, 101s, 101

22-, 26-, 28- and 30-gauge floral wires: green

Hydrangea leaf cutter: 4cm x 6cm (1½" x 2⅜") set of 2 (Sunflower Sugar Art)

SK-GI Hydrangea Leaf Veiner

Sandpaper

Template (see page 195)

Round cake stands:

   31cm (12") round x 10cm (4") tall
   26cm (10") round x 9.5cm (3¾") tall
   20cm (8") round x 9cm (3½") tall

Basket

1 Round off the edges of the smaller end of the polystyrene cone with sandpaper, then place it so the smaller, sandpapered end faces up. Brush with water then cover the whole column with green sugarpaste (see pages 33 to 34). Put each end in turn onto the template and use a cocktail stick to mark 32 equally spaced points around each end.

Tutor Tip

Make sure that you place the polystyrene exactly onto the circumference of the template of the same size.

2 To raise the base slightly, use a cocktail stick to fix a disc of polystyrene that is 1cm (³⁄₈") thick and smaller than 7cm (2¾") in diameter onto the larger end of the cone. Make sure that the cocktail stick is not sticking out from the polystyrene.

Tutor Tip

You can cut the disc of polystyrene from the cone used for the basket, or use a small lid or similar round object that is 1cm (³⁄₈") thick and smaller than 7cm (2³⁄₄") in diameter.

3 Place a sheet of greaseproof paper over the template and secure in place with a small amount of royal icing. Fit a piping bag with a no. 3 nozzle and fill with stiff-peak consistency royal icing (see page 25). Following the template, pipe the circumference of an 8.5cm (3³⁄₈") diameter circle onto the paper. Pipe a small amount of royal icing in the centre of the piped circle and place the larger end of the polystyrene cone directly on top of the piped circle and secure. Insert a sterilised dress pin into the top of the polystyrene at the point where you wish to start piping, using the marks made earlier as a guide.

4 Find the point on the piped circle that is directly below the dress pin, then count four marks to the right: this is where the first piped line will finish. Using stiff-peak

royal icing in a piping bag with a no. 5 nozzle, pipe a diagonal line of icing from the pin down towards the mark at the bottom. Carry on this way around the polystyrene, piping 32 parallel diagonal lines between the marks on the top and around the base of the polystyrene.

5 To create the basket-weave effect, start again from the pin and pipe another set of diagonal parallel lines around the polystyrene that cross over the first set, this time going from right to left.

6 Place some stiff-peak royal icing in a piping bag with a no. 3 nozzle. Use this

to pipe finer lines on top of the previous lines all the way around the basket and allow to dry. Do this in the same way as before, starting with all the left-to-right lines then adding the right-to-left lines.

7 Once the lines are completely dry, turn the polystyrene cone upside down and carefully remove the greaseproof paper. Use a no. 3 nozzle to pipe beads around the circumference of the smaller end of the cone. Using a no. 16 nozzle, pipe a rope around the larger end of the cone. When the piped rope is dry, remove the polystyrene disc you attached in step 2.

Hydrangeas

8 To make the flower bases, use sandpaper to round off the edges of a 6cm (2³⁄₈") and 5cm (2") polystyrene hemisphere. Tape three 22-gauge wires together with floral tape for each flower, leaving 2cm (¾") free at the end. Fold out the ends of the three wires to 90° so they are equally spaced in three different directions.

9 Use a no. 10 nozzle to pipe a large amount of green royal icing on the base of each polystyrene dome. Embed the wires into the icing and leave to dry. Holding the wires, use a palette knife to cover the whole piece of polystyrene with green royal icing and leave to dry again.

10 Before starting to pipe the hydrangeas, prepare some firm-peak royal icing and colour it as required so that it is ready to use. To give the hydrangeas a slightly two-tone effect, colour two slightly different bowls of icing with liquid food colours as follows:

Purple flowers: Prepare both purple and pinky-purple royal icing. When you pipe the flowers, place the nozzle required into a piping bag. Fill the bag with the two different colours.

Blue: Prepare blue and pinky-purple royal icing in a piping bag as above.

White: Prepare pale cream and yellow/green royal icing. When piping flower centres, put the two colours of royal icing in the same bag, as described above. Flowerets should be piped with pale cream icing.

Pink: These are piped with pink royal icing then lightly dusted purple when the flowers are dry.

Further instructions on piping flowers can be found on page 29.

11 Using a no. 14 nozzle and royal icing in the colour of your choice (as described above), pipe stars on top of the polystyrene base. In the same colour royal icing and with a no. 67 nozzle, pipe four-petal flowerets over the base until you have completely covered it and use a no. 1 nozzle to pipe the centres of the flowerets with the same icing. When they are dry, dust several petals with colours of your choice.

Leaves

12 Roll out some Holly/Ivy SFP, leave a mound for the wires and roll out further around the mound. Cut out with a hydrangea leaf cutter and use the hydrangea leaf veiner to add veins. Smooth the edge with a flower shaper and insert a green 28-gauge wire into the mound. Dust with Holly/Ivy dust food colour and use your fingers to shape each leaf and make them look more natural. Set aside to dry.

Flower balls

13 Use sandpaper to file down the base of a 3cm (1") polystyrene ball to make it flat. Tape three 26-gauge wires together with floral tape, leaving less than 1cm ($^5/_8$") free at the ends. Fold out the ends of the three wires to 90° so they are equally spaced and pointing in three different directions.

14 Use a no. 5 nozzle to pipe a mound of green royal icing onto the flat base of the polystyrene. Embed the wires into the royal icing and leave to dry. Holding the

wires, use a palette knife to cover the whole polystyrene ball with green royal icing and leave to dry.

15 Fit a piping bag with a no. 101 nozzle and fill with cream or blue royal icing. Pipe four-petal flowerets onto a flower nail (see page 29) and leave to dry. Use a no. 2 nozzle with green royal icing to stick the flowerets over the entire ball: you will need to make two balls covered with cream flowers and two with blue flowers for the arrangements on the top of this cake. Dust the centres of the flowerets: if the floweret is cream, dust with Vine food colour; if it is blue dust with Hydrangea food colour. Colour some royal icing yellow, fill a piping bag fitted with a no. 1 nozzle and pipe the centres of the cream flowerets. Pipe the centre of the blue flowerets with royal icing coloured with Hydrangea.

Floweret balls

16 Roll a small ball of Holly/Ivy SFP, insert a hooked green 30-gauge wire and leave to dry. Use a piping bag fitted with a no. 101s nozzle to pipe four-petal

flowerets in white or blue royal icing onto a flower nail and leave to dry. Use green royal icing to stick the flowerets over the whole polystyrene ball until it is completely covered. When the floweret balls are dry, tape two or three together with floral tape. Dust the white flowerets with Vine and the blue flowerets with Hydrangea.

Assembly

17 Use floral tape to bind each stem together with a thin and thick wire to make it strong enough to insert easily into the polystyrene.

18 Make holes in the top of the polystyrene basket with a bamboo skewer. Insert and fix the stems of the bouquet in the following order: hydrangea, large flower ball, small floweret ball and leaves.

Stand

19 Stack the cake stands so they are centred on top of each other. Place the mini cakes around the middle and lower tiers and the hydrangea basket on the top tier.

Hydrangea Mini Cakes

Edibles

Round mini cake (with ribbon): 5cm
(2") diameter x 4cm (1½") deep

40g (1½oz) sugarpaste/rolled fondant
per cake: white (SK)

50g (1¾oz) SK Instant Mix Royal Icing
per cake

Round mini cake (without ribbon): 5cm
(2") diameter x 3cm (1⅛") deep

35g (1¼oz) sugarpaste/rolled fondant
per cake: white (SK)

60g (2oz) SK Instant Mix Royal Icing
per cake

Seedless jam or buttercream

Equipment

Basic equipment (see pages 6 to 7)

Ribbon: 2cm (¾") wide x 18cm (7")
long for each cake

Piping nozzles: nos. 1, 67

Mini cakes with ribbon

1 Thinly spread jam or buttercream over
each mini cake, cover each with 40g
(1½oz) of white sugarpaste and leave to
stand for half a day until they are fully dry.
Wrap a ribbon around the bottom of the
cake and secure with a dab of royal icing
or edible glue. Use one hand to hold the
cake by the ribbon and with the other, use
a no. 67 nozzle to pipe four-petal flowerets
from the top of the cake to the top of the
ribbon (see page 29). With the same icing,
pipe dots in the centre of the flowerets with
a no. 1 piping nozzle.

Mini cakes without ribbon

2 Thinly spread jam or buttercream over
each mini cake, cover each with 35g
(1¼oz) of white sugarpaste and leave to
stand for half a day until they are is dry.
Attach a piece of greaseproof paper onto
a large flower nail with royal icing and
fix the mini cake onto the greaseproof
paper. Pipe four-petal flowerets with a no.
67 nozzle over the whole cake. Carefully
remove the cake and paper from the
flower nail and transfer to a plate to serve.

Tutor Tips

Coordinate the colour of the icing with the colour of the ribbon for a striking effect.

As royal icing dries quite hard, you can pipe the flowers onto the cakes with buttercream
rather than royal icing if you wish, see page 21.

Summer Splendour

(JULY)

Edibles

3 x round cakes:

  20cm (8") x 15cm (6") deep for bottom tier

  18cm (7") x 12cm (4½") deep for middle tier

  15cm (6") x 12cm (4½") deep for top tier

1.95kg (4lb 4¾oz) marzipan (SK)

1.95kg (4lb 4¾oz) sugarpaste/rolled fondant: white (SK)

50g (1¾oz) SK Sugar Florist Paste (SFP): White

300g (10½oz) SK Instant Mix Royal Icing

SK Designer Bridal Satin Lustre Dust Food Colour: White Satin

SK Designer Metallic Lustre Dust Food Colours: Classic Gold, Silver

SK Edible Glue

SK Gold Leaf Flake

Clear alcohol

Equipment

Basic equipment (see pages 6 to 7)

20.5cm, 18cm, 15cm (8", 7", 6") round cake boards

45cm, 35cm, 30cm, 25.5cm (18", 14", 12", 10") round acrylic boards

5-petal cutter: F10 (Orchard Products)

Rose petal cutters: 2cm x 3cm (¾" x 1⅛"), 1.5cm x 2cm (⅝" x ¾") (PME)

Piping nozzle: no. 0

Decoration

Eustoma, rose, Lantana and sweet pea sprays (see pages 116 to 123)

Covering the cakes

1 Place each cake onto a cake board of the same size. Cover the bottom tier with 850g (1lb 13oz) marzipan and 850g (1lb 13oz) white sugarpaste, the second tier with 600g (1lb 5¼oz) marzipan and 600g (1lb 5¼oz) white sugarpaste and the top tier with 500g (1lb 1¾oz) marzipan and 500g (1lb 1¾oz) white sugarpaste (see pages 30 to 34). Leave the cakes to stand for one day. Once dry, insert dowels in the bottom and second tiers (see page 38).

Decoration on the sides of the cakes

2 Mark a cross over the top of each cake to divide them into four parts. At the end of each of the crossed lines, follow the line down the side of the cake and make another mark. Draw a 'v' between two of these marks and use a leaf-shaping tool to define these lines: these will be the stalks for the floral decoration. Repeat around the cake, joining up the rest of the marks you have made.

3 Press rose petal cutters into the sugarpaste to make leaf shapes: place them so that the leaves appear to be growing out from the stalks. Use a leaf-shaping tool to draw lines in the centre of the shape the cutter has left and inscribe leaf veins into the paste.

4 Push a 5-petal cutter into the sugarpaste to make the flower patterns and use a bone tool to make dents in the centre of the flowers and the cake, bearing in mind which side will be the front of the cake as this final mark is where you will glue the decorative beetle.

Piped patterns

5 Use white royal icing and a no. 0 nozzle to pipe over the stalks and veins so that they stand out from the sugarpaste. Pipe dots around the petal shapes and allow to dry. Once the royal icing is dry, dust over the piped decoration with White Satin dust food colour.

Flowerets

6 Thinly roll out some White SFP and cut out a 5-petal flower using a cutter. Dust the paste with White Satin dust food colour and cup the petals with a bone tool. While they are still soft, attach the petals with edible glue to the centre of the iced flower outlines. Dust the centre of the flowers with Classic Gold dust food colour, pipe a dot in each centre with white royal icing and dust with White Satin dust food colour when dry.

Beetle

7 For the body, shape some sugarpaste into a cylinder that is 2.5cm x 1.2cm (1" x ⅝") long. Press a centre line into the body with a leaf-shaping tool. To make the beetle's head, shape more sugarpaste into a 2cm x 1cm (¾" x ⅜") cylinder. Sharpen one end of the cylinder into a thin point that is about 1cm (⅜") long.

8 Roll out a small amount of SFP on a board and make six thin sausages that are each 1.8cm (¾") in length. Use edible glue to glue the body and the head to the dent you made earlier in the cake. Use a ball tool to make three dents on either side of the body and attach the six legs.

9 Dissolve Silver dust food colour in alcohol and brush it over the beetle. Glue a gold leaf flake over the whole insect, pressing the leaf down softly with a dry paintbrush.

Cake assembly

Tutor Tip

When you secure the sprays around the cakes on acrylic boards, place each cake on a stand about 20.5cm (8") high and slightly larger than the acrylic boards.

10 Make the flowers for the sprays following the instructions on pages 118 to 123. Place the cakes in the centre of their respective acrylic boards and secure them in place with royal icing. Make several of sprays A, B and C (see page 123) and fasten to the 35cm (14") acrylic board using clear tape. Fasten sprays A and C to the 30.5cm (12") and 25cm (10") acrylic board, again using clear tape. Secure a spray of roses onto the top tier of the cake.

11 Place a 23cm (9") tall vase on a 45cm (18") round acrylic board and carefully stack the cakes on top of each other.

Summer Splendour

Mini Summer Cakes

Edibles

Round cakes:

10cm (4") x 10cm (4") deep

250g (9oz) marzipan for each cake (SK)

250g (9oz) white sugarpaste for each cake (SK)

5g (¼oz) SK Sugar Florist Paste (SFP): White for each cake

Equipment

Basic equipment (see pages 6 to 7)

10cm (4") cake card for each cake

Satin ribbon: 1.5cm (⅝") wide x 40cm (15²/₃") long cream

(See also the edibles and equipment for the larger Summer Splendour Cake)

These mini versions of the Summer Splendour Cake use the same materials as the large cake. This cake is ideal for a smaller wedding or to give to guests at the reception after the main event.

Tutor Tip

Avoid too much contact with the cake when you are arranging the flowers. To avoid any chance of ruining the delicate royal icing decorations, place the flowers around the cake rather than on it or put the sprays on an acetate sheet before you place them on the cake.

1 Use a small amount of royal icing to attach the cake to the cake card. Cover the cake with 250g (9oz) marzipan and then 250g (9oz) white sugarpaste. Divide the top of the cake into three and mark the three points with sterilised dress pins at the edge of the cake.

2 Use a leaf-shaping tool to draw vertical lines from the three pins down the sides of the cake. Press a rose petal cutter into the sugarpaste to make leaves on either side of the line. Cut out flower shapes from White SFP with a 5-petal cutter and glue them either side of the leaves.

3 Over-pipe the patterns with royal icing in the same manner as for the larger cake. Wrap cream ribbon around the base of the cake and stick down the ends with a small amount of royal icing. Place a smaller spray on top of the cake.

Double-flowered Eustoma

(LISIANTHUS)

Edibles

SK Sugar Florist Paste (SFP): Cream,
Pale Green, Pale Yellow

SK Designer Edible Pollen Dust Food
Colours: Apple Green, Pale Yellow

SK Designer Bridal Satin Lustre Dust
Food Colour: White Satin

SK Professional Dust Food Colour: Vine

SK Edible Glue

Equipment

Basic equipment (see page 8)

Peony cutter: 3.5cm x 6cm (1³/₈" x 2³/₈")
(Tinkertech)

Rose petal cutter: 2.5cm x 4cm
(1" x 1½") (PME)

Floral tape: green (half-width)

24-, 30-gauge floral wires: green

30-gauge floral wire: white

Tweezers

Flower centre

1 Make a tiny sausage of Pale Green
SFP for the pistil. Hold it horizontally and
insert a hooked 30-gauge green wire into
the bottom of the paste. Gently pinch
the sausage in the centre with a pair of
tweezers and allow to dry. Brush with
edible glue then dust with Apple Green
edible pollen food colour.

2 Roll some Pale Green SFP into a rugby
ball shape that is 1cm (³/₈") long. Attach it
about 1cm (³/₈") beneath the first piece of
paste on the wire and leave to dry.

3 Make six tiny balls of Pale Yellow SFP.
Insert a 30-gauge green wire into each
of the balls and leave to dry. Brush with
edible glue then dust with Pale Yellow
pollen dust food colour once they are dry.

4 Arrange the six stamens around the
pistil and secure with floral tape.

Petals

5 To make the inner petals, thinly roll out some Cream SFP and cut out five petals with a peony cutter. Add veins with a bamboo skewer and frill the edge of the petals with a bone tool. Dust the petals with White Satin and Vine dust food colours. Use your fingers to add movement to the petals and once they start to dry, glue them anti-clockwise around the pistil.

Tutor Tip

Glue the petals closely together so that they do not open out and spoil the shape of the flower.

6 For the outer petals, roll out some Cream SFP, insert a 30-gauge white wire and then roll out the paste around the wire to make it thinner. Cut out five petals with a peony cutter, shape and dust as for the inside petals. Attach the petals so they fit closely to the inside petals and secure with floral tape. Wrap the flower in foil to support it and leave to dry (see page 189).

7 Cut a piece of floral tape to about 6cm (2³/₈") long, cut one end into a point and pull the tape to curl it. Stick one of these to the back of each petal with edible glue to make the calyx and attach the floral tape to the neck of the flower with another piece of tape.

Buds

8 Roll a ball of Cream SFP into a thin teardrop shape. Insert a hooked 24-gauge green wire into the paste and leave to dry.

9 Thinly roll out some Cream SFP and cut out five petals with a rose petal cutter. Enlarge the petals a little by rolling over them with a CelPin and glue them around the SFP teardrop. Shape another four petals in the same way. Glue half of each petal to the cream centre and arrange the petals with your fingers for a more natural look. To give a natural shape, hold the edges of the petals and twist slightly.

10 Follow steps 8 and 9 for the outside petals and attach a calyx made of floral tape (see step 7).

Rose

Edibles

SK Sugar Florist Paste (SFP): Cream, Holly/Ivy

SK Designer Bridal Satin Lustre Dust Food Colour: White Satin

SK Edible Glue

Equipment

Basic equipment (see page 8)

2.8cm (1⅛") diameter polystyrene rose centre

22-gauge floral wire: green

Floral tape: green (half-width)

Rose petal cutter set (FMM):

  A: 4cm x 4.5cm (1½" x 1¾")

  B: 3.3cm x 3.5cm (1⅜" x 1⅜")

Rose petal cutter:

  C: 5cm x 5.8cm (2" x 2¼") (Sunflower Sugar Art)

Calyx cutter: R11C (Orchard Products)

Tutor Tips

The bottom of the petals should always be glued so that they are directly aligned with the wire.

If you prefer, you can make the rose centre from SFP rather than using polystyrene.

Flower

1 Insert a hooked, glued 22-gauge green wire into the polystyrene rose centre, secure and leave to dry (see page 185).

2 Thinly roll out some Cream SFP, cut with rose cutter B and turn the petal over so that the sharp edges are facing up. Use the curved side of rose cutter A to cut the petal about 2cm (¾") from the bottom. Brush edible glue over the top of the rose centre and wrap the petal around it.

Tutor Tip

Cutting a petal base with the curved end of a rose petal cutter makes the first petal shape easy to wrap around the flower centre.

3 Cut out two petals with rose cutter B. Curve the edges with a bone tool and dust with White Satin dust. Glue them alternately around the flower centre, slightly higher than the previous petal.

4 Cut out three more petals with rose cutter B, curve and dust as before. Attach them so that they are overlapping and sit slightly higher than the previous petals.

5 Cut out three petals with rose cutter A, curve and dust as before. Attach them in the same way as for the previous petals but open them up a little more.

6 Cut out three petals with rose cutter C and vein them with a veining tool. Curve the edges with a bone tool and curl them outward with a bamboo skewer. Cup the petals with a ball tool and leave them to one side to dry slightly. Whilst they are still pliable, dust them with White Satin dust and attach them between the previous petals, but position them so they sit slightly lower.

7 Cut out five petals with rose cutter C and repeat step 6. Arrange the petals at the base of the flower and stick them so about half the width of each petal overlaps.

8 Roll out some Holly/Ivy SFP and cut out with a calyx cutter. Stretch out the paste with a bone tool and make cuts up the edge of each sepal, as shown. To curl the calyx, draw the bone tool from the edges of the calyx petals to the centre. Turn the calyx over, insert the wire and attach the petals. Wrap floral tape around the wire, make a small ball with Holly/Ivy SFP and place it under the calyx to form a rosehip.

Buds

9 For the buds, follow the previous steps for making a rose but use nine petals rather than twelve. Attach a calyx and rosehip in the same way as for the full rose.

Tutor Tip

Adjust the size of a bud according to the number of petals used.

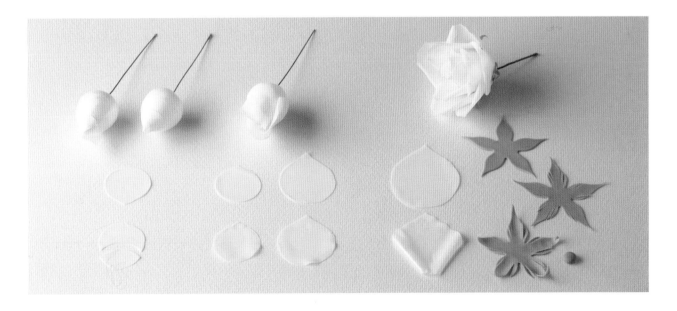

Ginger

Edibles

SK Sugar Florist Paste (SFP): White

SK Professional Dust Food Colours: Chestnut, Vine

SK Designer Bridal Satin Lustre Dust Food Colour: White Satin

SK Edible Glue

Equipment

Basic equipment (see page 8)

30-gauge floral wire: white

Floral tape: white (half-width)

Paper petal templates: A & B (see page 194)

Tutor Tip

All parts should be taped together before they dry out completely so that they are still pliable.

Pistil

1 Make a small ball of White SFP and insert a lightly glued wire. Place the ball on a board and roll it out with your fingers to make a thin sausage about 5cm (2") in length. Use a flower shaping tool to make a curve at one end of the paste and bend this to 45°. Dust the shaped part with Chestnut and Vine dust food colours and dust White Satin food colour over the neck.

Petals

2 Thinly roll out some more White SFP leaving a mound at the centre of the paste. Place template A over the paste so that the centre of the template is above the mound and cut around it with a cutting wheel. Insert a glued 30-gauge wire into the mound. Turn the template over and make another symmetrical petal in the same way.

3 Add veins to the petals by rolling a bamboo skewer over them. Curve the edges with a bone tool and dust with White Satin dust food colour. Repeat these steps to make four petals. Place the pistil between the symmetrical petals then wrap and secure with floral tape.

4 Follow steps 2 and 3 to make two petals with template B. Arrange and secure the two petals under the pistil with white floral tape.

Stamens

5 Make two sausages of White SFP and insert wires in the same way as for the pistil. Use a CelPin to stretch out the paste on either side of the wire and use a cutting wheel to make cuts in the paste that are 5cm–6cm (2"–2³/₈") in length to make stamens. Twist the tips of the stamens with your fingers and dust with White Satin and Vine dust food colours. Arrange them behind the flower and secure with floral tape.

Lantana

Edibles

SK Sugar Florist Paste (SFP): Holly/Ivy, White

SK Professional Dust Food Colours: Holly/Ivy, White

SK Edible Glue

SK Confectioners' Glaze

Equipment

Basic equipment (see page 8)

22-, 24-, 26-, 30-gauge floral wires: green

Floral tape: green (half-width)

Flower centre

1 Make a small ball of White SFP and insert a lightly glued 30-gauge wire into it.

2 Roll some SFP between your thumb and your index finger to make a thin sausage and then cut it in half. With a leaf-shaping tool, draw a central line down each sausage. Make five to six small sausages, bring them together and secure with floral tape.

Flowerets

3 For instructions on how to make flowerets, see the 'Flowerets' section in the English Rose Cake project, page 99. However, for this project you should use White SFP and make slits in four places. Arrange two to six flowerets around the flower centre and secure with floral tape.

Berries

4 Roll a small ball of Holly/Ivy SFP and insert a hooked 26-gauge wire. Make holes all over the surface of the ball with a cocktail stick and leave to dry. Roll a thin sausage of Holly/Ivy SFP and cut it into several pieces to form very small balls. Glue these onto the holes in the paste and cover them with confectioners' glaze when dry.

Leaves (optional for spray)

5 Roll out some Holly/Ivy SFP, leaving a mound for a wire, and then roll out even more thinly. Cut out a freehand leaf with a cutting wheel and insert a 30-gauge green wire into the mound. Vein the leaves with a leaf-shaping tool and dust with Vine dust food colour. Varnish with confectioners' glaze to finish. Use floral tape to alternately secure four to five leaves to a 24-gauge wire.

Assembly

6 Use the floral tape to secure the berries first and then the flowers to a 22-gauge wire. If you like, you can also secure leaves to the stem with floral tape.

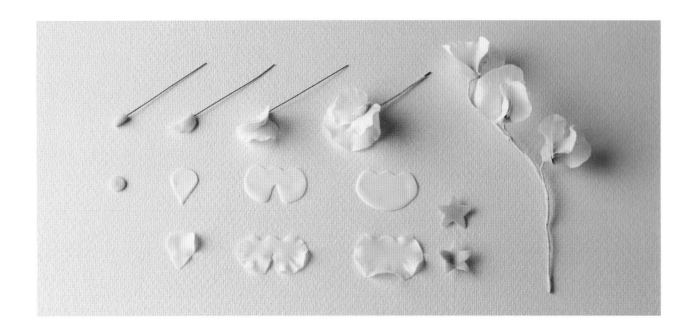

Sweet Pea

Edibles

SK Sugar Florist Paste (SFP): Cream, Pale Green

SK Professional Dust Food Colour: Vine

SK Edible Glue

Equipment

Basic equipment (see page 8)

Sweet pea cutter set (PME)

Rose petal cutter: 1.5cm x 2.3cm (⁵/₈" x 1") from set (PME)

24-, 26-, 32-gauge floral wires: green

Floral tape: pale green (half-width)

1 Make a small ball of Pale Green SFP and flatten it into a smooth circle with your thumb and index finger. Push a hooked 26-gauge wire into the centre, fold the paste in half and then leave to dry.

2 Thinly roll out some Cream SFP and cut with a rose petal cutter. Soften the edge of the petal with a bone tool, push it up the wire and secure it behind the ball of paste. Shape with scissors and bend the neck forward a little with tweezers.

3 Roll out some more Cream SFP and cut out both the inside and outside petals. Vein with a bamboo skewer and frill the edges with a bone tool. Glue the inside petals behind the first petal and leave to dry. Glue the outside petals behind the first petals, shape with your fingers and tape them to the wire.

4 Make another small ball of Pale Green SFP. Flatten with your thumb and index finger in the same way as before and press it against the small hole of a sponge pad. Roll out thinly around the bump in the centre of the paste and cut with a star-shaped cutter. Put the paste on a board and press the centre with a bone tool to cup. Smooth the edges of the star and insert a wire from underneath. Secure at the base of the petals to form the calyx.

5 Attach two to three flowers to a 24-gauge wire with floral tape. Wrap a thin wire around a bamboo skewer to curl it, remove and attach it to a stem with floral tape.

Assembly of Sprays

Equipment

Bear grass and artificial leaves

Floral tape: green (full-width)

Tutor Tip

When assembling flowers into a spray, place dried leaves between the sugar flowers so as not to damage them.

1 For spray A, bring together the Lantana and the double-flowered Eustoma (Lisianthus), fill out with artificial leaves in-between and secure with floral tape. Add a long stem of artificial leaves and secure with floral tape.

2 To make spray B, arrange the flowers in the following order: sweet peas, rose buds, a rose, and a ginger flower. Fill out with artificial leaves in-between, then secure with floral tape.

3 For spray C, arrange the flowers in the following order: rose buds, a rose and a ginger flower. Fill out with artificial leaves and secure with floral tape.

4 Make as many sprays as required to go around all three cakes. Avoid contact with the cake by placing the flowers around it rather than on it, or put the sprays onto acetate sheets and then place them on top of each cake.

Tropical Wedding Cake

(AUGUST)

Edibles

2 x round cakes:

25.5cm (10") x 15cm (6") for bottom tier

15cm (6") x 11cm (4¼") for top tier

2kg (4lb 6½oz) marzipan (SK)

2.9kg (6lb 6½oz) sugarpaste/rolled fondant: white (SK)

500g (1lb ¾oz) SK Instant Mix Royal icing with added glucose/corn syrup (see page 25): 150g (5¼oz) coloured with Holly/Ivy paste food colour, 150g (5¼oz) coloured with Holly/Ivy and Mint (Christmas green) paste food colours, 200g (7oz) coloured with Daffodil (yellow) paste food colour

SK Professional Paste Food Colours: Daffodil (yellow), Holly/Ivy, Mint (Christmas green), Vine

SK Professional Dust Food Colours: Mint (Christmas green), Vine

Clear alcohol

Equipment

Basic equipment (see pages 6 to 7)

Round cake drums: 2 x 20.5cm (8"), 1 x 33cm (13")

Round cake boards: 15cm, 25.5cm (6", 10")

Round cake cards: 10cm, 20.5cm (4", 8")

Satin ribbon: 2.5cm (1") wide x 2.3m (91") long deep green, 1.5cm (½") wide x 1.1m (43½") long deep green

20-gauge floral wire: green

Floral tape: green (full-width)

Long, pointed tweezers

Acetate sheet (or a piping bag fitted with no. 2 piping nozzle)

Cruciform acrylic pillar: 15.5cm x 16.5cm (6" x 6½")

Round cake stand, at least 15.5cm (6") tall

3 posy picks

Decoration

Phalaenopsis and Oncidium Orchids (see pages 130 to 133)

Tutor Tip

Before you start, it is a good idea to draw out the pale green palm leaves as a guideline for the cake decoration on a spare piece of rolled out sugarpaste.

Cake drum

1 Cover the 33cm (13") cake drum with 900g (2lb) white sugarpaste (see page 35) and leave to dry for several days. Glue the 1.5cm (½") wide dark green satin ribbon around the edge of the drum.

2 Mix Vine and Mint dust food colours separately with clear alcohol and use to paint palm leaves onto the covered cake drum with a round paintbrush. Starting from the centre of the drum and moving outwards, paint approximately six leaves with Vine food colour as shown in the picture on page 127. To finish, paint over the Vine-coloured leaves with Mint food colour to give them more depth.

3 Stick two 20.5cm (8") cake drums together with a non-toxic glue stick and attach the 2.5cm (1") wide dark green ribbon around the edge of the drums. Use royal icing to secure the 20.5cm (8") drums to the centre of the larger drum.

Bottom tier

4 Level the top of the larger cake with a sharp knife to give it a flat surface. Place a 20.5cm (8") cake card centrally on top of the cake. Insert cocktail sticks at 5cm (2") intervals around the sides of the cake, about 3cm (1¹/₈") down from the top of the cake. Using a sharp knife, cut away the cake between the cocktail sticks and the edge of the cake card to make the top of the cake domed. Remove the cake card and the cocktail sticks and secure the cake onto a 25.5cm (10") cake board with royal icing.

5 First cover the cake with 1.5kg (3lb 5oz) marzipan, then cover with 1.5kg (3lb 5oz) of white sugarpaste (see pages 30 to 34) and leave to dry for one day. Use a cocktail stick to make five marks on the top of the cake: one at the centre and four at points 6cm (2³/₈") diagonally from the centre to make a cross shape. For

more guidance on how to mark a cake, see page 37.

6 Insert cake dowels at each of the five marks and cut to size (see page 38). The dowels should sit higher than the cake but should not come higher than the sugarpaste. Place the cruciform acrylic pillar so that it sits on top of the dowels. Press the pillar down into the sugarpaste until it meets the dowels and marks the paste, then remove the pillar and put to one side for later.

7 Paint palm leaves over the cake in the same way as for the cake drum and then pipe tropical leaf patterns over the four parts of the cake as explained below. Leave the pattern to dry overnight.

8 Once the icing has dried, attach a 2.5cm (1") wide dark green ribbon around the bottom of the cake. Use royal icing to secure the cake to the centre of the smaller cake drum.

Piped leaf patterns

9 Prepare some dark green, pale green, and yellow royal icing with added glucose syrup (corn syrup) and pipe the two tiers

as described below. For more guidance on how to colour the icing refer to the leaf cookies on page 134.

> **Tutor Tip**
>
> If the royal icing is too soft to pipe the stems, add a little more icing/confectioners' sugar until you achieve the right consistency.

10 For the stems, mark several lines in the sugarpaste with a leaf shaping tool, working downwards from the top of the cake. Mark small leaves on either side of the stems and fill any gaps in the pattern with bigger leaves to make a balanced design. Working again from the top of the cake downwards, paint the tropical leaves in the same way as for the cake drum on page 124.

11 Use an acetate sheet as a piping bag or fit a paper piping bag with a no. 2 nozzle and fill with pale green royal icing with added glucose/corn syrup (see page 25). Pipe along the lines for the stems. For the small leaves, pipe the veins following steps 1 to 3 for Cookie A, page 134. For the larger leaves, pipe

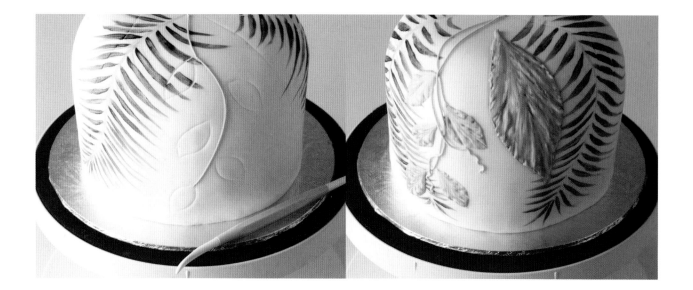

the veins following steps 1 to 3 for Cookie B. Use pale green royal icing and a no. 2 piping nozzle to pipe vines overlapping the stems.

Top tier

12 Level the top of the smaller cake with a sharp knife to give it a flat surface. Place a 10cm (4") cake card centrally on top of the cake. Repeat step 4 to make the top tier cake dome-shaped, as for the bottom tier. Place the 15cm (6") cake on a cake board of the same size, cover with 500g (1lb 1¾oz) marzipan, then cover with 500g (1lb 1¾oz) of white sugarpaste. Leave the cake to dry for a day then insert three posy picks towards the back of the cake.

13 Divide the surface of the cake into three equal parts and make marks at these points. Paint and pipe the same tropical leaf pattern as before over the three sections of the cake. Once the icing has dried, attach a 2.5cm (1") wide green ribbon around the bottom of the cake.

14 Make the orchids for the top tier following the instructions on pages 130 to 133. Use green floral tape to bind together stems of three Phalaenopsis orchids, with

a long-stemmed orchid at the centre. Prepare two long-stemmed Oncidium orchids and several other shorter Oncidium stems. Make several U-shaped pins from 20-gauge floral wire.

15 Place the cake on a stand of the same height as the pillar or higher to arrange the flowers on the cake (see page 191 for full instructions on securing a large bouquet on a cake). Arrange the flowers so that their weight is evenly spread across the top of the cake; by doing so the bouquet should stay stable. Pinch the stems together with two or three U-shaped wire pins and secure the bouquet into the posy picks. Place a long-stemmed Oncidium either side of the bouquet and secure into the picks. Secure other Oncidium orchids into the picks, bearing in mind the overall appearance of the spray.

Assembly

16 Fit the acrylic cruciform pillar into the dents on top of the bottom tier cake. Place the top tier cake and board onto the pillar. Tape together three Phalaenopsis orchids with green floral tape and place on the lower tier to finish.

Tropical Wedding Cake

Phalaenopsis Orchid

Edibles

SK Sugar Florist Paste (SFP): Pale Pink, Pale Yellow, White

SK Professional Paste Food Colours: Poinsettia (Christmas red), Rose

SK Professional Dust Food Colours: Cyclamen, Daffodil (yellow), Poinsettia (Christmas red), Rose

SK Designer Bridal Satin Dust Food Colour: White Satin

SK Edible Glue

Clear alcohol

Equipment

Basic equipment (see page 8)

24-, 30-gauge floral wires: white

20-gauge floral wires: green

Phalaenopsis Orchid cutter: labellum (lip) 4.5cm x 5cm (1¾" x 2") (Tinkertech)

Floral tape: white, green (half-width)

Cotton thread: red

Tweezers

Templates, see page 195

Tutor Tip

Tape each petal, except for the labellum, with floral tape before it is dry so that the finished flower will not lose its shape.

Preparation

1 Prepare three kinds of pink SFP as follows:

Dark pink: add a small amount of Rose paste food colour to Pale Pink SFP;

Reddish pink: add a small amount of Poinsettia paste food colour to Pale Pink SFP;

Pale pink: mix some Pale Pink SFP with White SFP.

2 Make dark pink and pale pink Phalaenopsis orchids with the following coloured flower paste and dust colours:

Dark pink Phalaenopsis: make the side petals and sepals from the dark pink paste and dust with Rose and Poinsettia dust food colours. Make the labellum from the reddish pink paste and dust with Poinsettia dust food colour.

Pale pink Phalaenopsis: make the side petals and sepals from the pale pink paste and dust with Rose and White Satin dust food colours. Make the labellum from the dark pink paste and dust with Poinsettia dust food colour.

Labellum

3 Cover a piece of red cotton thread with glue and leave to dry. Once dry, cut to 4cm (1½") long and stroke with your fingers to curl.

4 Thinly roll out some SFP in your desired colour for the labellum, leaving a mound for the wire. When you place the cutter over the paste, the length of the mound should reach about ¾ of the way up the petal from the rounded end. Cut the paste with the Phalaenopsis labellum cutter, making sure that the mound is central. Smooth the edge with a flower-shaping tool. Remember that the sharp

pointed end will be the outer tip of the labellum.

5 Cut off the rounded end of the labellum to make it straight and insert a 30-gauge wire into the mound. Turn over and dust with Poinsettia dust food colour: this will be the upper side of the labellum.

6 Lift the end of the labellum, nip the point where the wire enters the paste with a pair of pointed tweezers and bend the wire forward to 90°. Next, at about 3mm (¹/₈") below the point where the wire enters the mound, bend the wire backwards by 180°. Use tweezers to bend and fold the wire into position. Make a small ball of White SFP and attach at the bend in the wire.

7 Dust Daffodil food colour at the centre of the labellum and attach a small ball of Pale Yellow SFP to it. Mix some Cyclamen dust food colour with clear alcohol and, using a fine paintbrush,

paint dots at the centre of the petal then paint around the edges. Brush edible glue 1cm (³/₈") above the pointed edge of the labellum, place the glued cotton thread across the paste and fold back the point with the thread in between. Pinch the centre with your fingers from underneath. Lift the round petals on both sides with your fingers. Make a ring out of tissue paper, place it around the flower as a support and remove when dry.

Side petals

8 Thinly roll out some SFP in the desired colour, leaving a mound for the wire. Vein either side of the mound with a veining tool. Place the template over the paste, ensuring that the centre of the template is over the mound, and cut out the petal with a cutting wheel. Turn the template over and cut out another symmetrical petal in the same way. Insert a 30-gauge wire into the mound, smooth

the petal edges with a flower-shaping tool and dust them with the appropriate colour.

9 Curve the tips of the petals inward and tape them together with white floral tape, so that the dusted sides of the petals face up. Place the labellum between the side petals and tape them all together with white floral tape.

Sepals

10 Thinly roll out some SFP in the desired colour, leaving a mound for the wire. Place the template over the paste, ensuring that the centre of the template is over the mound, and cut out one of Sepal A and two of Sepal B with a cutting wheel. Insert the wire into the mound and make a line on either side of the mound with a leaf-shaping tool. Smooth the petal with a flower-shaping tool and dust with the appropriate dust colour. Tape the first sepal centrally behind the side petals. Place the other two sepals on either side of the flower so they are slightly lower than the petals and secure with white floral tape.

11 Make a small ball with SFP in the colour of the flower, push it up the taped wires and secure at the base of the flower.

Buds

12 Make a large teardrop from SFP in the desired colour, insert a hooked 24-gauge white wire into the bottom of the teardrop and leave to dry.

13 Using SFP in the desired colour, make a sausage the same length as the teardrop and taper both ends. Place a CelPin on the centre of the sausage, roll across the width a little and make a central line with a leaf-shaping tool. Make three of these sausages and glue them to the teardrop with the central lines facing inwards. Dust with the appropriate dust food colour.

Assembly

14 Dust Rose food colour over the floral tape at the base of the flower.

15 Using green floral tape, tape 2–3 buds to the end of a 20-gauge green wire and then tape another 5–6 flowers along it, one by one. Make sure to tape the buds and flowers 2cm (¾") down from the end of each wire. Adjust the length of the stem according to the number of flowers. Lift the bases of the individual flowers with tweezers in order to turn them right and left alternately, starting from the tip of the stem.

Oncidium Orchid

Edibles

SK Sugar Florist Paste (SFP): Pale Green, Pale Yellow

SK Professional Dust Food Colours: Cyclamen, Daffodil (yellow), Vine

SK Edible Glue

Clear alcohol

Equipment

Basic equipment (see page 8)

30-, 22-gauge floral wires: white

Oncidium Orchid cutter (Tinkertech)

6-petal cutters: no. 6 (2cm/¾"), no. 8 (9mm/³/₈") (Orchard Products)

Floral tape: green (half-width)

Tutor Tip

If you would prefer to make pink Oncidium orchids rather than yellow, make the flowers using Pale Pink SFP instead.

Flower

1 Thinly roll out some Pale Yellow SFP, leaving a mound for the wire, and cut with an Oncidium cutter. Insert a white 30-gauge wire into the mound and frill the edge of the petal with a bone tool. Dust the whole flower with Daffodil food colour and dust Vine food colour just at the centre. Cup the flower and bend the wire back behind the petal.

2 Roll out some Pale Green SFP and cut out with the no. 6 six-petal cutter, then cut the flower shape in half. Mix some Cyclamen dust food colour with clear alcohol and use a fine paintbrush to dot the colour in the centre of the cupped petal. Use the same colour to paint horizontal stripes across the half flower. Glue the half flower underneath the flower, with the stripes pointing in an upward direction.

3 Roll out some more Pale Yellow SFP and cut out a no. 8 six-petal cutter. Cup the petals with a bone tool. Stick this at the centre of the flower with a little edible glue.

Buds

4 Make a small ball of Pale Green SFP and insert a 30-gauge hooked wire and leave to dry.

5 Roll out some Pale Yellow SFP, cut out with a no. 6 six-petal cutter and cup with a bone tool. Push the yellow flower up the wire so it sits behind the ball of green SFP. Stick the petals of the flower to the green SFP alternately, with three facing inward and three facing outward. Use Cyclamen dust food colour mixed with clear alcohol to paint horizontal stripes onto the petals with a fine paintbrush. This will be the smallest bud. Repeat to make 3–4 buds per stem.

Assembly

6 Wrap green floral tape around the stem of each bud and flower.

7 Start to create the trailing stem by taping 2–3 buds together, one behind the other. Take one of the smallest buds, which will be the tip of the stem, and tape another small bud to the wire of this using green floral tape. After you have taped a few buds together, tape the wire of the last bud to a 22-gauge wire to lengthen the stem. Tape about 5–6 buds and flowers along the wire, behind the smallest buds at the tip.

8 Tape several of these long stems together, bending each one to shape, to make a stem of the desired length.

Leaf Cookies

Edibles

Cookies cut into leaf shapes (see recipe on page 16)

Royal icing with added glucose/corn syrup, coloured as for the Tropical Wedding Cake (see page 124)

Equipment

Acetate piping bags (or greaseproof piping bags with no. 2 piping nozzle)

Preparation

1 Bake two different leaf-shaped cookies using cutters of your choice.

2 Colour the three batches of royal icing with added glucose/corn syrup as follows:

Green: Holly/Ivy paste food colour;

Dark green: Holly/Ivy and Mint paste colours;

Yellow: Daffodil paste colour.

3 Make three acetate piping bags, or use paper piping bags fitted with a no. 2 nozzle if you prefer.

4 Fill three bags half-full with the different colours of royal icing and firmly close the ends. If you are using acetate piping bags, cut off the tip to the size of a no. 2 piping nozzle just before you pipe.

Piping leaf vein patterns

Cookie A

1 Pipe a line around the edge of the cookie with green royal icing and added glucose/corn syrup.

2 With the same green royal icing and added glucose/corn syrup, pipe parallel lines across the leaf from the tip to ¾ along the cookie. These lines should not run over the line around the edge. Pipe yellow lines between the first green lines.

3 Starting from the tip, pull down the icing with a damp cocktail stick to make a central line on the leaf. Pull the icing from the edges in towards the central line and from the central line down to the base. Pull a cocktail stick through the icing in several places to make the vein pattern and leave to dry.

Cookie B

1 Pipe a line around the edge of the cookie using dark green royal icing with added glucose/corn syrup.

2 Starting at the edges, pipe lines with the same icing across the leaf, leaving a small gap between each line. End each line a little above the base and pipe yellow lines between the green lines.

3 With a damp cocktail stick, pull the icing from the tip of the leaf to the base. To make the vein pattern, pull the icing in several places from the tip of the leaf down to the base and leave to dry.

Café-au-Lait Wedding Cake

(SEPTEMBER)

Edibles

4 x round cakes:

  28cm (11") x 10cm (3") deep for bottom tier

  23cm (9") x 10cm (3") deep for first tier

  18cm (7") x 10cm (3") deep for second tier

  15cm (6") x 8cm (3") deep for top tier

3.22kg (7lb ¾oz) marzipan (SK)

Sugarpaste/rolled fondant: 2.22kg (4lb 13½oz) white, 1.5kg (3lb 5oz) cream, 1kg (2lb 3¼oz) beige (white coloured with a touch of Chestnut paste food colour) (SK)

Modelling paste:

  700g (1lb 8¾oz) white = 420g (15oz) White SFP + 280g (10oz) white sugarpaste

SK Instant Mix Royal Icing

SK Designer Bridal Satin Lustre Dust Food Colour: White Satin

SK Edible Glue

Equipment

Basic equipment (see pages 6 to 7)

Round cake drums: 48cm (19"), 2 x 25.5cm (10")

Round cake boards: 28cm, 23cm, 18cm, 15cm (11", 9", 7", 6")

Satin ribbon: 2.5cm (1") wide x 85cm (33") long and 1.5cm (⅝") wide x 1.55m (61") long pale pink

Decoration

White, cream, and salmon pink dahlias (see pages 142 to 143)

Covering the cake drums

1 Mix 1kg (2lb ¾oz) of cream sugarpaste and 500g (1lb 1¾oz) of beige sugarpaste to create a marbled pattern. Roll out the marbled sugarpaste, cover the 48cm (19") cake drum and leave to dry for several days. Attach a length of pale pink satin ribbon around the edge of the drum with either a non-toxic glue stick or double-sided tape.

2 Stick two 25.5cm (10") cake drums together with a non-toxic glue stick and attach a length of pale pink satin ribbon around the edge of the drums. Use royal icing to secure these boards on top of the larger board so that they sit off-centre, about 3cm (1⅛") to the right.

3 Secure all the cakes onto cake boards of the same size and cover them with marzipan (see pages 30 to 34). You will need 1.3kg (2lb 13¾oz) of marzipan for the bottom tier; 880g (1lb 15¼oz) for the

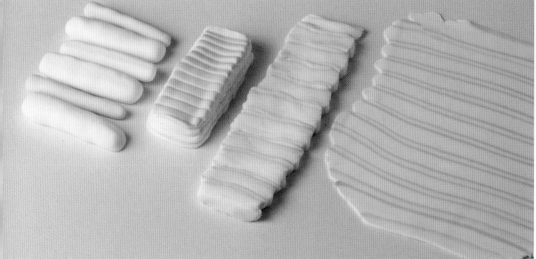

first tier; 600g (1lb 5¼oz) for the second tier; and 440g (15½oz) of marzipan for the top tier.

Covering the cakes

4 To cover each cake you will need to weigh out quantities of sugarpaste in white, beige and cream. Divide each amount of white sugarpaste into thirds and the beige sugarpaste in half. Roll all the pieces of sugarpaste into sausages as follows:

Bottom tier: 900g (2lb) white, 200g (7oz) beige, 200g (7oz) cream. Roll to 18cm (7") long.

First tier: 600g (1lb 5¼oz) white, 140g (5oz) beige, 140g (5oz) cream. Roll to 16cm (6") long.

Second tier: 420g (14¾oz) white, 90g (3oz) beige, 90g (3oz) cream. Roll to 15cm (6") long.

Top tier: 300g (10½oz) white, 70g (2½oz) beige, 70g (2½oz) cream. Roll to 13cm (5") long.

5 Using a rolling pin, roll out the white sugarpaste sausages into rectangles that are 5mm (¼") thick. Roll out the beige and cream sausages into rectangles of the same size, but thinner than the white rectangles. Layer the rectangles on top of each other as follows (from the bottom): white, beige, white, cream, white, beige.

6 Slice across the short side of the stacked rectangles at 1cm (³/₈") intervals. Roll the sliced paste onto its side, tightly line up the slices to make striped bands and place in the centre of a non-stick board. Use a rolling pin to stretch the paste up and down in the direction of the stripes. If the paste is not wide enough, stretch the paste from side-to-side as well.

7 Cover the cakes with this paste (see pages 30 to 33). Use a smoother to help stick the paste in place so that the joins in the paste do not split. When the surface of the paste is dry, insert the cake dowels into the three lower tiers (see instructions on page 38).

Drapes: bottom and first tiers

8 Secure the bottom tier in the centre of the 25.5cm (10") cake drum and secure the first tier centrally on top of the bottom tier using royal icing.

9 Insert dress pins that have been sterilised in alcohol into the top left-hand side of the bottom tier and the top right-hand side of the first tier. Wind cotton thread around the cake, starting from the dress pin on the first tier, going under the pin on the bottom tier, round the other side of the cake and coming back over the pin in the first tier again. Tie the thread in a bow.

10 Cut a piece of aluminium foil so that it is 20cm–25cm (8"–10") wide and about 20cm (8") long. Fold the top edge of the foil over by about 2cm (¾") and hook it over the thread. Raise the lower edge of the foil and support with polystyrene or kitchen paper, as shown in the picture.

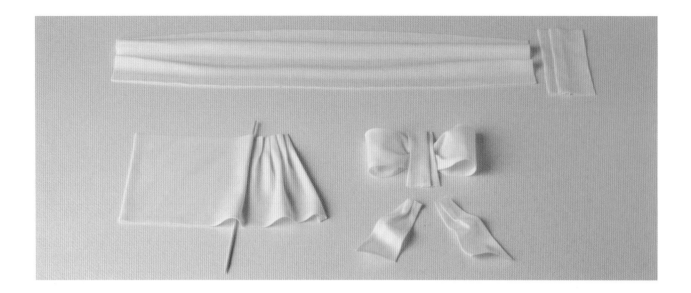

11 To make the fabric-effect drapes, roll out some white modelling paste (see table below) to about 13cm (5") wide and 2mm–3mm (1/8") thick. Cut one side of the width straight and put it through a pasta machine widthways several times. Change the dial from 1 up to 9 to make a thin, long band of paste. If you don't have a pasta machine, roll the paste thinly on a non-stick board greased with white vegetable fat to prevent sticking. Cut the band exactly to the length shown below, fold back the edges of the band a little and dust with White Satin dust food colour.

12 Make drape A following the instructions above. Gather and ruche the paste on one side until it is about 7cm (2¾") wide and use a bamboo skewer under the paste to lift the edge.

13 Glue the band to the side of the cake with edible glue, starting 2cm (¾") above the dress pin in the bottom tier and 2cm (¾") above the aluminium foil. Make approximately 12 drapes to go around the whole cake and glue them about 2cm (¾") short of the dress pins on the bottom and first tiers.

Tutor Tip

Any joins should face inwards so that the band looks as if it is all one piece of paste.

14 Remove the dress pin from the bottom tier and glue a ruched drape into the space where the pin has been removed. Remove the dress pin from the first tier, pull one end of the bow to untie the thread and remove it from the cake. Glue another ruched drape into the space where the pin has been removed. When the ruffles around the cake are dry and firm, remove the aluminium foil.

15 Make two of drape B and use your fingers to make loose folds along the paste. Glue the draped bands so that they cover the top edge of the gathered drapes around the cake.

16 Cut out a 9cm (3½") square from the leftover modelling paste from which the two B drapes were cut. Make a drape with one dart, gently fold back the top and bottom and glue this at the join.

Tutor Tip

Wrap any leftover paste in cling film and use it to make the next band.

	White modelling paste	Length	Width
First Tier	Drape A 30g (1oz)	25cm (10")	13cm (5")
	Drape B 50g (1¾oz)	40cm (16")	13cm (5")
	Drape C 40g (1½oz)	30cm (12")	12cm (4¾")
Second Tier	Drape D 45g (1½oz)	35cm (14")	13cm (5")
Top Tier	Drape E 60g (2oz)	45cm (18")	13cm (5")
	Drape F 26g (1oz)	15cm (6")	12cm (4¾")

Drapes: second and top tiers

17 Insert a posy pick into the middle of the top tier, then secure the second tier onto the first and the top tier onto the second with royal icing.

18 Make a drape with the measurements for band D. Glue it onto the side of the second tier, starting from the bottom right and finishing at the top left of the cake.

19 Make a drape with the measurements for band E. Glue this onto the side of the top tier: start from the bottom of the top tier, going behind the cake, coming up to the front of the top of the cake and ending at the left of the posy pick. Make another square from the trimmings, pleat and secure over the join as for the lower tier.

20 Make drape F and cut in half along the length of the paste. Pleat one of the pieces, glue it to the right of the posy pick on the top tier and arrange the end of the drape hanging down towards the right side of the cake. Make a ring with the other half and cover the join with the pleated square. Glue the ring onto drape E on the top tier with the ring facing left.

Bow

21 Make drape C according to the instructions and cut in half widthways. Make a loop with one band by joining the ends at the back and twisting a little with your fingers, then repeat to make a second loop. Roll out another drape, cut a rectangle 7cm x 6cm (2¾" x 2⅜") and pleat to make a knot. Place it at the centre of the bow and secure both ends at the back of the bow. Support the bow with tissue paper.

22 Using the leftover paste from the bow, cut a 20cm x 4cm (8" x 1½") rectangular piece of paste and cut in half lengthways. Gather one end with your fingers and cut the other end diagonally. Curve the paste and support with tissue paper. Before the bow and the ribbon ends are firm, glue the ends then the bow to the point at which the draped bands cross over the first and second tiers.

Dahlias

23 Secure a single dahlia into the posy pick on the top tier. Make a small ball of sugarpaste and glue it onto the cake drum to the right of the bottom tier. Insert two dahlias into the sugarpaste. Make sure this paste, the posy pick and the dahlias are removed before the cake is served.

Dahlia

Edibles

SK Sugar Florist Paste (SFP): Cream, Pale Pink, Pale Yellow, White

SK Professional Dust Food Colours: Rose, Vine

SK Designer Bridal Satin Lustre Dust Food Colour: White Satin

SK Edible Glue

Tutor Tip

Wrap and secure the petals to the stem as soon as they are made, then arrange the petals with your fingers so that they are not uniform and look more natural.

Equipment

Basic equipment (see page 8)

20-gauge green and 30-gauge white floral wires

Cutters:

  A 5cm (2") 6-petal cutter (Orchard Products)

  B 2.5cm x 4cm (1" x 1½") rose cutter from set of 4 (PME)

  C 1.3cm x 4cm (⅝" x 1½") orchid calyx cutter (Kit Box: set of 2, small)

  D 2.2cm x 4.6cm (¾" x 2") lily cutter (Kit Box: set of 2, small)

  E 2cm x 6cm (¾" x 2⅜") lily cutter (Kit Box: from set of 2, medium)

  F 2.6cm x 8.1cm (1" x 2¾") lily cutter (Kit Box: from set of 2, large)

Flower centre

1 Make a ball of White, Cream or Pale Pink SFP 2cm (¾") in diameter. Insert a green 20-gauge hooked wire and set aside to dry.

2 Thinly roll out some SFP and cut out three sets of petals with cutter A. Use a bone tool to stretch each petal vertically, cut halfway along the length of each petal with a cutting wheel and curl the tip towards the centre using a bone tool. Push the wire through the petals and attach them to the SFP ball: wrap the first one tightly and keep the second and the third gradually more open.

3 Thinly roll out more SFP and cut out another set of petals with cutter A. Stretch the length of each petal slightly, vein them with a bamboo skewer and glue underneath the first petals. Dust the petals with White Satin, Vine and Rose dust food colours to make them appear more realistic.

Inner petals

4 Thinly roll out more SFP and cut out seven petals with cutter B and ten petals with cutter C with the pointed end of the cutter facing upwards. Stretch the width of each petal with a CelStick, vein with a bamboo skewer and make a central line with a leaf-shaping tool. Curl each petal towards the centre with a bone tool and dust as before. Attach the petals from cutter B around the flower centre petals and then attach the ten petals from cutter C around those seven.

Outer petals

5 Thinly roll out some SFP and cut into two pieces. Place a white 30-gauge wire on one piece and lay the other piece on top so that the wire is sandwiched in between the two. Roll out the paste around the wire even more thinly and cut out a petal shape. You will need to make to make six to eight wired petals with cutter D, and 12 each of cutters E and F. Shape and dust in the same way as for the other petals but do not curl the base. Curve the wire from the base to top of the petals with your fingers.

6 Tape the wired petals to the flower around the existing petals in the following order:

Six to eight petals cut with D;

Six petals cut with E;

Six petals cut with F;

Six petals cut with F (point the petal tip outwards slightly);

Six petals cut with E (point the petal tip down).

To finish

7 Make extra petals and add them to the flower where necessary, bearing in mind the balance of the cake as a whole. Add a little extra dust colour to the petals if needed: dust Rose dust food colour on the top and sides of all the petals and Vine dust food colour on the base.

Ruffles and Frills Anemone Cake

(OCTOBER)

Edibles

2 x round cakes: 20.5cm (8") x 10cm (4") deep

1.7kg (3lb 8½oz) marzipan (SK)

2.55kg (5lb 8¼oz) sugarpaste: white (SK)

Modelling paste:

500g (1lb 1¾oz) white = 350g (12¼oz) White SFP + 150g (5¼oz) white sugarpaste

200g (7oz) pink = 140g (5oz) Pale Pink SFP + 60g (2oz) white sugarpaste

200g (7oz) purple = 140g (5oz) Soft Lilac SFP + 60g (2oz) white sugarpaste

Small amount of SK Instant Mix Royal Icing

SK Designer Bridal Satin Lustre Dust Food Colour: White Satin

SK Edible Glue

Equipment

Basic equipment (see pages 6 to 7)

2 x 20.5cm (8") round cake boards

25.5cm (10") round cake drum

13cm (5") round cake card

Satin ribbon: 1.5cm (⅝") wide x 85cm (33½") long white

Round cutters: 15cm, 12cm, 10cm, 6cm, 5cm, 4cm (6", 5", 4", 2⅜", 2", 1½")

30.5cm (12") round cake stand

Decoration

Anemone spray, see pages 152 to 153

Cake drum

1 Cover the cake drum with 850g (1lb 13oz) of white sugarpaste (see page 35). Leave it to dry for several days then attach a length of white satin ribbon around the edge of the drum with a non-toxic glue stick or double-sided tape.

Top tier

2 Trim off the top of the cake with a sharp knife to give it a flat surface and place a 12.5cm (5") cake card centrally on top of the cake. Insert cocktail sticks at 5cm–6cm (2"–2¼") intervals around the sides of the cake, approximately 5cm (2") down from the top. Using a sharp knife, cut away the cake between the cocktail sticks and the edge of the cake card to make the top of the cake domed. When you have an even shape, remove the cake card and the cocktail sticks.

3 Secure the 20.5cm (8") cake onto the cake board of the same size. Cover

first with 850g (1lb 13oz) of marzipan and then with 850g (1lb 13oz) of white sugarpaste (see pages 30 to 34) and leave it to dry for a day.

Bottom tier

4 Trim the top of the cake with a sharp knife to give the cake a flat surface, then trim around the bottom edge of the cake at a slight angle. Cover the cake with 850g (1lb 13oz) marzipan and then with 850g (1lb 13oz) white sugarpaste. Secure the cake to the centre of the 20.5cm (10") cake drum, then insert cake dowels to support the upper tier (see page 38). Secure the first cake on top of the bottom tier with royal icing.

Making frills

5 To make frill rings for this cake you will need the following cutters:

10cm (4") round cutter, with a 4cm (1½") diameter central hole

12cm (5") round cutter, with a 5cm (2") diameter central hole

15cm (6") round cutter, with a 6cm (2½") diameter central hole

15cm (6") round cutter with a 5cm (2") diameter central hole

Prepare the white, pink and purple modelling pastes. Thinly roll out the pastes, place a round cutter on the paste and cut out a circle with a cutting wheel to make a neat edge. Place a smaller cutter on the circle of paste, as above, but do not cut through the paste. Dust White Satin food colour over the paste left outside the cutter. Dust the reverse side in the same way and flare the edge of the paste with a ball tool.

Tutor Tips

The size of each frill is proportional to the size of the round cutter that you are using.

The amount of modelling paste you need will vary according to the design and the arrangement of the frills.

6 Lightly fold the circle of paste into quarters to make a piping bag shape. Place the round cutter for the central hole at the tip of the fold and cut. Unfold the paste and to make a ring: this will be the base for all the following frill patterns used on this cake.

7 Single band: Make a single cut in the ring of paste from the edge to the central hole. Hold the cut ends of the ring with both hands and fold the paste loosely over itself to make a ruffled vertical band.

8 Double band: Make several rings of the same size and in different colours. Overlap them loosely and follow the same steps for making a single band.

9 Rose: Use a 10cm (4") or 12cm (5") round cutter to make a frill ring then cut through the paste and open it out slightly. Make a pleat about 1/3 from one end to start off the rose centre. Start rolling from that point towards the remaining 2/3. Roll tightly at the beginning and gradually allow the rolls to become looser until the frill resembles a rose shape.

10 Single cluster: For this cluster frill, do not cut the ring of paste. Fold the ring in

half and gather the paste loosely but offset it so that the edges aren't together. Pick it up and fold the paste gently from side to side.

11 Double clusters: Make several rings of the same size and in different colours. Do the same as for the single cluster, but fold the paste so that the offset edges of the paste are visible.

12 Crescent shape: Make several rings of the same size but in different colours. Fold each ring in half and place them on top of each other, making sure that the edges of each ring overhang each other a little. Make a tuck in the paste and bring the ends together so that the central holes are no longer visible.

13 Gathered frill: Fold a ring in half and softly fold the paste approximately 2cm (¾") from the edge of the ring. Do this the whole way around the ring.

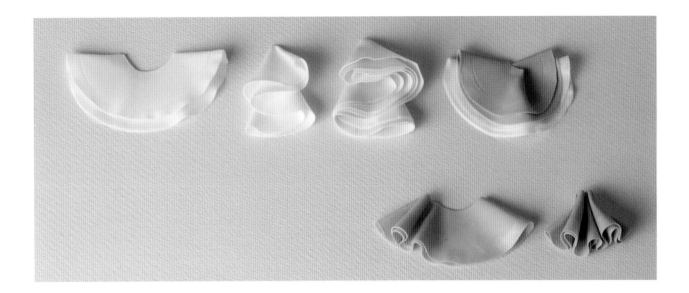

Attaching the cake frills

Tutor Tips

You can follow the guidelines here or choose the colour, size, and pattern of the frills to suit your own or your recipient's taste.

Attach larger frills to the cake first and then stick smaller frills where you need to fill any gaps. Attach the frills to the cake as soon as they are made so that the paste is still pliable and overlap the frills with your fingers to give the cake a natural appearance.

Tuck small pieces of kitchen paper underneath the frills until they firm up so that they keep their shape.

Make sure that you space the frills evenly around the whole cake.

14 Use a 10cm (4") round cutter with a 4cm (1½") central hole to make gathered frills with white modelling paste and arrange them around the bottom of the cake.

15 Thinly roll out some white modelling paste and use a 15cm (6") round cutter with a central hole that is 6cm (2½") diameter to make several flared bands with a single cut in the ring that are 5cm (2") wide (see opposite). Glue them towards the top of the first tier, making sure that you position upward-facing frills all the way round the cake. Overlap the frills carefully so that the joins are hidden.

16 Use a 15cm (6") round cutter with a 5cm (2") diameter central hole to make several larger flares and attach these above the previous bands. Cut out some white modelling paste with a 10cm (4") round cutter, fold the circle in half and roll to make a cone shape. Repeat to make several cones and glue them underneath the flares to support them.

Cake assembly

17 Place the cake on the cake stand and arrange the anemone spray on top.

Anemone

Edibles

SK Sugar Florist Paste (SFP): Soft Lilac

SK Professional Dust Food Colours: Lilac, Violet

SK Edible Glue

Equipment

Basic equipment (see page 8)

30-gauge floral wires: white

Floral tape: green (half-width and full-width)

Cotton thread: purple

Rose cutters: 3.5cm x 4.5cm (1³/₈" x 1¾"), 4cm x 5cm (1½" x 2") (Tinkertech)

Satin ribbon: short length of white or purple (for tying the flower stems)

Flowers

1 Bend a 30-gauge white wire in half then twist the wire at the bend to make a small loop.

2 Wind purple cotton thread about 50 times around your index, middle, and fourth fingers. Cut the thread from the reel and remove it from your fingers. Twist the thread once in the middle to make a figure of eight, fold one ring over the other and pass one end of the wire through the ring. Twist the wires once or twice beneath the thread to hold it in place, leaving the small loop in the wire made in step 1, then twist the wires together down the length to make them into one. Splay out the cotton loops then cut through them all. Cover the ends of the cotton with edible glue then dust with Violet and Lilac dust food colours.

Tutor Tip

Make the desired dusting colour by mixing Violet and Lilac dust food colours together.

Ruffles and Frills Anemone Cake

3 Roll some Soft Lilac SFP into a 1cm (³/₈") diameter ball to make the flower centre. Insert a cocktail stick into the centre of the paste, cover the ball with edible glue and dust with Violet and Lilac dust food colours. Insert another cocktail stick into the side of the flower centre to pick it up and attach the ball to the small loop of wire at the centre of the thread.

4 Roll some Soft Lilac SFP into a rugby ball shape, insert a 30-gauge white wire and roll out the paste away from you with a rolling pin. Roll out further around the wire and cut out a thin leaf shape that is 4cm–5cm (1½"–2") long. Dust Violet and Lilac food colours at the base of the leaf shape and cut two deep slits in the paste, either side of the wire. Use a bone tool to

arch the cut paste away from the central piece of paste. Fit to the flower centre and secure with floral tape.

5 Roll out some more Soft Lilac SFP, insert a wire and roll out the paste further around the wire. Cut with the 3.5cm x 4.5cm (1³/₈" x 1¾") rose cutter and vein the petal with a bamboo skewer. Dust Violet and Lilac dust food colours at the base of the petal and smooth the edge with a flower shaping tool. Place it with the flower centre and tape in position.

6 Repeat the previous steps to make four inner petals and tape them in place. Make five or six more petals and use floral tape to tape them around the inner petals as outer petals.

Seven-flower anemone spray

7 Make seven anemones following the instructions above. As soon as the first

Tutor Tip

Tape each flower to the bouquet one by one as it is made and before it dries out. By doing so, the bouquet will have a tight, neat finish.

flower is finished, bend the neck upward a little.

8 Do the same with the next flower and tape it to the first one.

9 Tape the third flower to the second flower and raise it up above the other flowers.

10 Attach each flower to the one before, raising each one up slightly to make the bouquet dome-shaped.

11 Bring the wire stems together, then tie a satin ribbon around them in a bow.

Tutor Tip

Once you have made each petal, immediately attach it to the flower centre whilst the paste is still soft.

Bird of Joy Wedding Cake

(NOVEMBER)

Edibles

2 x square cakes:

25.5cm (10") x 12.5cm (5") deep for bottom tier

18cm (7") x 10cm (4") deep for middle tier

2.55kg (5lb 8¼oz) marzipan (SK)

3.5kg (7lb 9½oz) sugarpaste/rolled fondant: 2.55kg (5lb 8¼oz) white coloured with a touch of Chestnut paste food colour, 950g (2lb 1¼oz) green (SK)

Modelling paste:

500g (1lb 1¾oz) white = 200g (7oz) White SFP + 240g (8½oz) white sugarpaste

250g (8¾oz) beige = 100g (3½oz) Soft Peach SFP + 150g (5¼oz) white sugarpaste

100g (3½oz) green = 40g (1½oz) Holly/Ivy SFP + 60g (2oz) white sugarpaste

300g (10½oz) SK Instant Mix Royal Icing

SK Professional Paste Food Colours: Leaf Green, Rose

SK Professional Dust Food Colour: Rose

SK Designer Bridal Satin Lustre Dust Food Colours: Chiffon Pink, White Satin

SK Edible Glue

White vegetable fat/shortening

Clear alcohol

Equipment

Basic equipment (see pages 6 to 7)

38cm (15") square cake drum

Square cake boards: 25.5cm, 18cm (10", 7")

Satin ribbons: 1.5cm (⅝") wide x 1.6m (63") long green and dark green

Pasta machine (optional)

Piping nozzles: nos. 1, 2

Small rose petal cutter, from set of four (PME)

Lace leaf cutters: small, medium (Orchard Products)

Bead makers: 3mm, 8mm (⅛", ¼")

Rose pattern texture mat from set of 6 floral designs (Autumn Carpenter)

Straight frill cutter (FMM)

Diagonal pattern textured rolling pin

Sponge

Decoration

Bird and birdcage, see pages 162 to 165

Preparation

1 Add a little Rose paste food colour to the beige sugarpaste and the beige modelling paste to make them a light pinky-beige colour.

Cake drum

2 Cover the square cake drum with 950g (2lb 1¼oz) of green sugarpaste (see page 35) and leave it to dry for several days.

3 Attach a length of dark green satin ribbon around the top of the edge of the cake drum, then attach a lighter green satin ribbon around the bottom of the edge of the cake drum so that it overlaps the dark green ribbon, leaving a small amount of the deep green ribbon visible.

Bottom tier

4 Secure the largest cake onto a cake board of the same size. Cover it first with

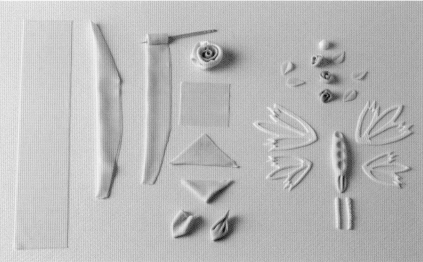

1.7kg (4lb) marzipan then with 1.7kg (4lb) of pinky-beige sugarpaste (see pages 30 to 34). Secure the cake to the centre of the cake drum and insert cake dowels to support the upper tiers (see page 38). Make a central mark at the bottom of each side of the cake; these four marks are where the lace ribbons will be attached.

Middle tier

5 Secure the middle tier cake onto a cake board of the same size and cover with 850g (1lb 13oz) of marzipan and then 850g (1lb 13oz) of pinky-beige sugarpaste. Mark the position of the cake dowels within the circumference of the cake stand base (see page 37) and insert them into the cake. Secure the cake centrally on top of the bottom tier.

Lace dragonflies

6 Thinly roll out some white modelling paste and emboss it with a textured rolling pin. To make the wings for one dragonfly, cut out two pieces of paste with the small lace leaf cutter and two pieces with the medium lace leaf cutter. Dust all four

pieces with White Satin lustre dust and leave to dry.

7 Dust the bead maker with White Satin lustre dust food colour, make a stick of white modelling paste and press this into the dusted bead maker. Remove the paste from the maker and trim any excess paste with a cutting wheel. Use the same paste to make a larger 8mm (¼") pearl for the dragonfly's head and to make two strands of pearls that are eight 3mm (⅛") pearls long for the tail. Leave to dry.

8 Roll out some pinky-beige modelling paste and cut out a 5cm x 4cm (2" x 1½") rectangle. Make three small satin ribbon roses following the instructions on page 160. Roll out some green modelling paste and cut out 5–6 leaves with a small rose cutter. Mark a central line in each leaf using a leaf-shaping tool.

9 Make a 5cm (2") sausage with pinky-beige modelling paste. Round off one end of the paste, which will be the head, and taper the other end to form the dragonfly's body. Dent this paste in four places with the end of a CelPin. Using a leaf-shaping tool, make two marks near each end of the body. Use edible glue to attach the

8mm (¼") pearl to the mark for the head and attach a strand of eight 3mm (⅛") pearls to the mark at the end of the body. Attach the roses and leaves to the dents in between with edible glue.

10 Make a notch on each side of the body with a leaf-shaping tool. Use edible glue to attach the small wing to the lower notch and the medium-sized wing to the upper notch with glue. Support the wings in place with tissue paper and leave to dry. Repeat these steps to create a second dragonfly.

Lace ribbons

11 Thinly roll out some white modelling paste and make a long strip that is 8cm (3⅛") wide. From this piece of paste cut strips with two different widths, so they are either 5cm (2") or 3cm (1⅛") wide.

12 Lightly grease the textured side of a rose pattern texture mat with white vegetable fat. Place a strip of paste that is 5cm (2") wide onto the mat and press down with a sponge to imprint the pattern onto the paste. Fold back the longer edges by 5mm (⅛").

13 Cut along the longer edges of the 3cm (1¹⁄₈") wide paste with a straight frill cutter. When you do this, make sure the patterns on the top and bottom are symmetrical. Punch three holes into the top of each frill using a no. 2 piping nozzle and cut along the length of the paste to make two bands. Glue the straight edge of one band to the folded edge of the textured paste to create a ribbon and repeat along the opposite edge. Turn the ribbon over and dust with White Satin food colour.

Tutor Tip

A pasta machine is convenient for making a long strip of paste, see page 90. However, if you do not have a pasta machine you can simply roll the paste out thinly on a non-stick board greased with white vegetable fat.

14 Following the steps above, make eight lengths of lace ribbon for the bottom tier. Take the first ribbon and cut one end on the diagonal. Glue the edge of this end across the mark you made earlier on the side of the cake. Glue this ribbon diagonally across the side of the cake and stick it down above the corner. Repeat for the second ribbon, gluing it so that it crosses over and is symmetrical to the first ribbon. Repeat this on the other three sides of the bottom tier. Join the ends of each pair of ribbons on the top of the cake and trim off the excess.

Tutor Tip

Attach the ribbon to the cake before it is dry.

15 Using white royal icing and a no. 1 nozzle, pipe over the embossed rose pattern on the ribbons and allow to dry. Mix White Satin dust food colour with clear alcohol and paint over the roses on the ribbon when the icing has dried.

Tutor Tip

You will find it easier to pipe intricate patterns if you loosen the consistency of the royal icing by adding a little cooled, boiled water.

16 For the middle tier, make four lace ribbons that are 24cm (9½") long. Take the first ribbon and cut one end on the diagonal and repeat for the second ribbon symmetrically. Use a paintbrush to brush edible glue at the bottom left corners of the cake and stick the cut ends of the two ribbons so that they overlap each other; the two ribbons should look like they are a continuation of the ribbons on the bottom tier. Glue the ribbons diagonally across the side of the cake and stick them down above the corners. Turn the cake around so that the back is towards you and repeat the same method with two other ribbons. Join the ends of the two ribbons on the top of the cake as before and trim neatly.

17 Using white royal icing and a no. 1 nozzle, pipe over the embossed rose pattern on the ribbon as before and allow to dry. Dust the roses with White Satin dust food colour mixed with clear alcohol once the icing has dried.

Bow

18 Use white modelling paste to make a lace ribbon that is 22cm (8½") long. Cut both ends diagonally so that you are left

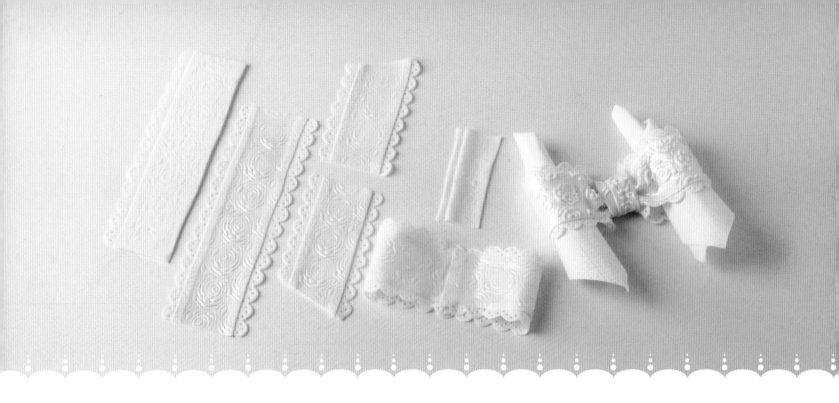

with a trapezium shape. At the cut edges, fold a very small amount of the paste over to the back so that you are left with a neat edge. Cut the ribbons in half and glue them on the corners of the cake where the lace ribbons cross over. Pipe over the embossed rose pattern on the ribbon as before, then dust the roses with White Satin dust food colour mixed with clear alcohol once the icing has dried.

19 For the bow loops, make a ribbon that is 25.5cm (10") long. Make it into a loop and join both ends with edible glue. Lightly pinch the centre of the ring with your fingers to make a bow shape.

20 Make a band of paste measuring 8cm x 5cm (3¹/₈" x 2") and slightly fold back the longer sides of the paste to make a neat edge. Pinch a dart along the middle of the band. Fold this paste around the centre of the bow and join the ends together at the back to form the knot.

21 Support the bow with tissue paper, over-pipe with royal icing and dust the dried pattern with White Satin dust as before.

22 Roll a small ball of sugarpaste and attach it to the back of the bow. Use edible glue to stick the bow to the bow

ends that you previously attached to the cake. Make one more complete bow and glue it on the opposite corner of the cake where the lace ribbons cross over.

Satin ribbon and rose decoration

23 Thinly roll out some pinky-beige modelling paste and make a rectangle that is 20cm x 4cm (8" x 1½") in size. Dust one side of the paste with Chiffon Pink and Rose dust food colours. Gently fold the paste in half lengthways, taking care not to make a crease. Cut the ends of the paste into points.

24 Starting at one end, wind the paste around a cocktail stick, making sure the pointed ends are facing downwards. Keep turning the cocktail stick until you get halfway along the paste. As you wind the rest of the paste, make loose frills with your fingers as you go to form a rose.

25 For the leaves, add Leaf Green paste food colour to 100g (3½oz) of white modelling paste. Thinly roll out the paste and cut a 4cm (1½") square. Fold

the square into a triangle, then fold it again to make into another smaller triangle. With the longer side at the bottom, fold the right and left corners in and pinch them in the centre with your fingers.

26 For the bottom tier, roll out some pinky-beige modelling paste and cut out four strips measuring 4cm x 27cm (1½" x 10½"). For the middle tier, roll out more pinky-beige modelling paste and cut four strips measuring 4cm x 23cm (1½" x 9").

27 Slightly fold back the longer sides of the paste to make a neat edge. Dust the colour of your choice over the top of the paste. Moving along the ribbon, use your fingers to pinch and gather the paste at 7cm (2¾") intervals.

Tutor Tip

You can dust the ribbon and roses using any of the dust colours you have already used on the cake.

28 Attach the 27cm (11") long ribbons above the white lace ribbon on the front and back of the bottom tier. Next, attach the 23cm (9") ribbons below the white lace

ribbons on the middle tier. Finally, attach the remaining ribbons in the same way to the other sides of the cake. Join the ends of the ribbons together on top of the middle tier and trim off the excess.

29 Roll out more pinky-beige modelling paste and make two strips measuring 4cm x 10cm (1½" x 4"). Fold the lengths in half and glue them where the ends of the satin ribbons meet. Before the strips are dry, secure the lace dragonflies on top with edible glue (see page 158). Before the ribbon roses and leaves are dry, use edible glue to stick them to the gathers of the ribbons.

Shirring ribbon

Tutor Tip

To make a shirring ribbon, ensure that the band of paste you start with is 2½ times the desired length of the shirring ribbon you need.

30 Thinly roll out white modelling paste into a long strip that is 3.5cm (1³⁄₈") wide. The length of the paste will vary according to its use. Cut along the longer edges with a straight frill cutter and use a no. 2 nozzle to punch holes in the ribbon. Dust with White Satin dust food colour.

31 Hold one of the longer edges with a cocktail stick and gather the paste little by little. Place the gathered paste onto a foam pad and put a ruler along the middle of the length of paste, then press it down whilst lifting the paste up on either side.

32 Glue the shirring ribbon all the way around the bottom tier. It is easier to make a small piece of the ribbon at a time and then glue it down as you go. Make the last shirring ribbon from a piece of paste that is twice the length of the gap you need to fill.

Top tier

33 Make the bird and birdcage as explained on pages 162 to 164. Roll a ball of sugarpaste and secure it to the bottom of the cage with edible glue. Firmly secure the bird onto this ball of sugarpaste.

34 Place the small cake stand centrally on the middle tier and place the birdcage on the stand.

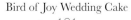

Bird and Birdcage

Edibles

Hexagonal cake or dummy: 12cm (5") x
10cm (4") deep

250g (8¾oz) marzipan (SK)

450g (1lb) sugarpaste: green (SK)

Modelling paste:

  100g (3½oz) white = 60g (2oz) White
  SFP + 40g (1½oz) white sugarpaste

50g (1¾oz) SK Instant Mix Royal Icing

SK Designer Bridal Satin Lustre Dust Food
Colours: Delphinium, Lavender, White
Satin

SK Designer Metallic Lustre Dust Food
Colour: Light Gold

SK Professional Dust Food Colour: Rose

Gelatine 'gemstone': green (see page 173)

SK Edible Glue

Clear alcohol

Equipment

Basic equipment (see pages 6 to 7)

15cm x 3cm (6" x 1¹/₈") hexagonal
polystyrene base

2cm (¾") polystyrene ball

Piping nozzle: no. 4

30-gauge floral wire: white

4mm (¹/₈") bead maker

Thin striped textured rolling pin (Sunflower
Sugar Art)

Embosser of your choice

8mm (¼") round cutter

10cm (4") round x 5cm (2") tall cake
stand: green

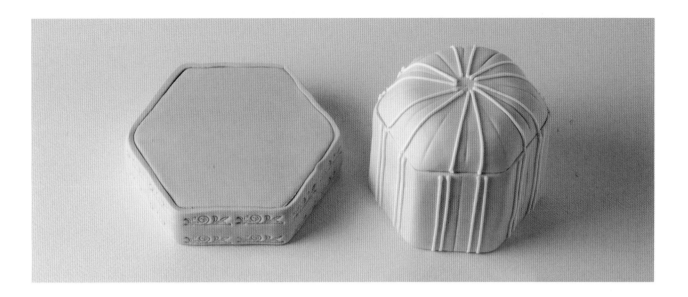

Base

1 Cover the top and sides of the hexagonal polystyrene base with 200g (7oz) of green sugarpaste. Cover the top first and then cover the sides with a band of paste measuring 3.5cm (1³/₈") wide x 46cm (18") long. Emboss patterns around the sides of the hexagon whilst the paste is still soft, then leave to dry fully. Paint over the pattern with Light Gold dust food colour mixed with clear alcohol.

Birdcage

2 Place an 8cm (3¹/₈") round cutter centrally on top of the cake and mark around its circumference. Use royal icing or a cocktail stick to make marks 2cm (¾") down the sides of the cake. Cut the cake between the marks on the top and the sides of the cake to make the top of the cake dome-shaped.

3 To cover the cake you will need 250g (8¾oz) each of marzipan and green sugarpaste. Cover the domed part with marzipan and trim away the excess. Roll out the remaining marzipan and cut out two 8cm x 16.5cm (3¹/₈" x 6½") rectangles. Glue these marzipan

rectangles onto the sides of the cake. Cover the cake with green sugarpaste in the same way.

4 Mark five points at the top and bottom edges on each side of the cake as follows: first mark the centre of each side; then make marks 1cm (³/₈") either side of the central mark; then mark 5mm (¹/₈") outside the second marks. Use a ruler to join up the marks on the top and the bottom of each side with five vertical, parallel lines. Draw lines between the three central marks on the top edge of the cake and the top of the dome to create the roof of the bird cage. Using white royal icing in a piping bag with a no. 4 nozzle, pipe along the lines you have made, excluding the central lines. Paint over the iced lines with White Satin dust mixed with clear alcohol once they are dry.

5 Using a 4mm (¹/₈") bead maker and white modelling paste, make six strands of pearl beads that are 8cm (3¹/₈") long and six strands that are 6cm (2³/₈") long. Stick these strands of pearls over the central lines that have not been piped over. The longer strands should be stuck to the sides of the birdcage and the shorter strands should be used for the top.

6 Make six 8cm (3¹/₈") shirring ribbons as explained on page 161: you will need an 18cm (3¹/₈") band of paste to make each ribbon. Glue these ribbons down each corner of the cake.

7 Make eighteen 6cm (2³/₈") shirring ribbons: you will need a 14cm (5½") band of paste for each ribbon. Glue six ribbons over the dome, from the top of the cake sides to the top of the dome. Glue twelve ribbons horizontally around the top and bottom of the cake.

8 Cover the 2cm (¾") polystyrene ball with sugarpaste and divide it into eight (see pages 172 to 173 of the Christmas Couture Cake for more guidance). Make eight strands of 4mm (¹/₈") pearl beads from white sugarpaste, glue them around the ball and secure it at the top of the dome.

Bird

Important note

The bird contains a wire so must be removed from the cake before it is served. Make sure the recipient of the cake is aware that the bird is inedible and must not be eaten.

9 To make the head and body of the bird, take 20g (¾oz) of white modelling paste and make a fat sausage approximately 7cm (2¾") long. Lift one end and pull out a small head shape. Thinly roll out some more white modelling paste and texture it with a textured rolling pin. Cut the textured paste a little larger than the bird's body, cover the body with the paste and stick it down neatly at the back of the bird. Form a small beak with your fingers.

10 Make dents on either side of the head with the end of a paintbrush. Attach a gelatine dot to the dent with edible glue (see page 173, step 7 of the Christmas Baubles for how to make gelatine dots).

11 For the tail, roll a ball of white modelling paste and insert a glued 30-gauge wire. Roll the paste around the wire and make it into a 5.5cm (2¼") sausage.

12 To make a feather, thinly roll out some white modelling paste and then use a textured rolling pin to emboss thin stripes onto the paste. Cut to the required length and make cuts in the paste with a cutting wheel. For the tail, make a feather that is about 2.5cm (1") wide and 6cm (2⅜") long. Glue the feather to the wire and attach the wire to the body as a tail.

13 Make a feather that is 3cm (1⅛") x 7cm (2¾") in size and glue it onto the back of the body and halfway along the tail so that it is overlapping the tail feathers.

14 For the wing, make a 1.5cm x 3.5cm (½" x 1⅜") wing-shaped base out of white modelling paste. Thinly roll out some more white modelling paste and texture with the same rolling pin as you used for the tail. Cut the paste slightly larger than the base, make cuts in the lower half of the paste and cover the base with the textured paste. Glue this to the side of the body.

15 To make the crown, roll a small amount of modelling paste with your fingers and make a thin sausage approximately 2.5cm (1") long. Press the centre of the sausage with a sterilised dress pin to make it 'v'-shaped. Stick a dress pin into the 'v' shape and use the pin to carry it to the bird's head. Glue in place. Repeat to make several 'v' shapes and secure them all to the head.

16 Paint the beak, crown and the feathers using Light Gold dust mixed with clear alcohol. Dust the body with Delphinium and Lavender dust food colours, then dust the bird's cheeks and chest with Rose dust food colour.

Tutor Tip

Make sure the bird is completely dry before you attach it to the cage.

Christmas Couture Cake

(DECEMBER)

Edibles

20.5cm (8") x 7.5cm (3") square cake

20.5cm (8") x 7cm (2¾") round cake

15cm (6") x 6cm (2½") hexagonal cake

2.2kg (4lb 8oz) marzipan (SK)

3.6kg (7lb 8½oz) sugarpaste: 2.2kg (4lb 8oz) blue, 1.4kg (3lb ½oz) white (SK)

300g (10½oz) SK Instant Mix Royal Icing

SK Professional Liquid Food Colours: Mint, Bluebell, Rose

SK Designer Bridal Satin Lustre Dust Food Colours: Damask Rose, Lavender, Myrtle, White Satin

SK Designer Moon Beam Dust Food Colour: Jade

SK Designer Metallic Lustre Dust Food Colour: Light Gold

SK Sugar Diamonds: 1.4cm (⅝")

SK Edible Glue

Clear alcohol

Equipment

Basic equipment (see pages 6 to 7)

33cm (13") square cake drum

Round cake boards: 13cm, 20.5cm (5", 8")

Satin ribbon: 1.5cm (⅝") wide x 1.1m (43¼") long champagne colour

90cm (35½") cotton thread

Piping nozzles: nos. 0, 3, 101s

Decoration

Christmas tree and baubles, see pages 172 to 177

Cake drum

1 Cover the cake drum with 900g (2lb) of white sugarpaste (see page 35) and leave to dry. Dust the surface with White Satin dust food colour and glue a length of champagne-coloured satin ribbon around the edge using a non-toxic glue stick or double-sided tape.

Bottom tier

2 Cover the cake with 1kg (2lb ¾oz) of marzipan (see pages 30 to 34), then cover with 1kg (2lb ¾oz) of blue sugarpaste and leave overnight. Bear in mind that the 20.5cm (8") round cake for the middle tier will sit approximately 4cm (1½") from the right edge of this bottom tier and insert the cake dowels accordingly (see page 38).

3 Use a ruler to draw diagonal lines from the centre of the cake to the bottom corners with a quilting wheel. Draw parallel lines 3cm (1⅛") apart and draw crossover lines in the same manner. Mix some Myrtle

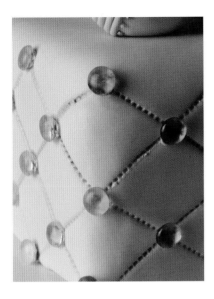

dust food colour with clear alcohol and use this to paint the quilting lines with a fine paintbrush. Make up a bag of Mint-coloured royal icing and snip off the tip of the bag. Pipe dots on the points at which the lines cross and glue sugar diamonds here.

Middle tier

4 Fix the 20.5cm (8") round cake onto a cake board of the same size. Cover the cake with 800g (1lb 1¾oz) of marzipan, then cover with 800g (1lb 1¾oz) of blue sugarpaste and leave overnight. Insert the cake dowels into this tier, bearing in mind that the 15cm (6") hexagonal top tier cake will be placed towards the left side of this cake (see page 36).

5 Half-insert sterilised glass-headed dress pins in several places around the cake so they are 3.5cm (1³/₈") from the bottom. Wrap a length of cotton around the cake level with the dress pins. Cut the thread, leaving about 10cm (4") surplus at both ends. Cross over the ends using both hands and pull firmly to mark a horizontal line around the cake. Safely remove the cotton and all of the

pins. Use a 7cm (2¾") round cutter to mark curved lines above and below the central line made with the thread.

Tutor Tip

It is a good idea to count the pins as you insert them into the cake, so that you know how many you should have when you take them out.

6 Use a piping bag fitted with a no. 3 nozzle to pipe 2–3 lines of Mint-coloured royal icing along the central line and the curved lines above and below. Use a no. 0 nozzle to pipe blue and pink (Bluebell and Rose) royal icing dots at the ends of the curved lines; the dots should decrease in size as you pipe towards the edges of the cake. Once the icing is dry, mix Damask Rose, Myrtle and Lavender lustre dust colours with alcohol and use a fine paintbrush to paint over the dots.

Top tier

7 Fix the 15cm (6") hexagonal cake onto a cake board of the same size. Cover the

cake with 400g (10½oz) marzipan, then cover with 400g (14oz) blue sugarpaste. Leave it to dry for a few hours and insert dowels into the cake (see page 38).

8 Mark the centre of each side of the hexagonal cake, then mark 1cm (³/₈") from either side of the first mark. Using these marks, draw seven vertical lines down the cake.

Piped patterns

9 Column of flowerets: Use a no. 101s nozzle with dark and pale blue royal icing to pipe five-petal blossoms onto wax paper and allow to dry. When dry, pipe a vertical line with green royal icing through the central mark on each of the sides. Glue the flowerets to the line with the same icing. On either side of this piped line, go over the vertical lines with a quilting wheel. Mix Myrtle lustre dust food colour with clear alcohol and use a fine paintbrush to paint over the lines.

10 Flower clusters: Use a piping bag fitted with a no. 0 nozzle to pipe vertical lines of green royal icing through the lines on one side of the lines you made

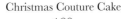

with a quilting wheel. Pipe a number of blue dots with a no. 0 nozzle to make a flower cluster. When they are dry, mix some Lavender lustre dust food colour with clear alcohol and paint with a fine paintbrush. Use a no. 0 nozzle to pipe leaves with the green-coloured royal icing.

11 Column of dots: Use a no. 0 nozzle to pipe vertical lines with white royal icing on the marks either side of the column of flower clusters. Pipe large and small dots alternately down each side of the lines and, when dry, mix White Satin and Light Gold lustre dust colours with clear alcohol and paint the dots with a fine paintbrush.

Cake assembly

12 Make the baubles and Christmas tree according to the instructions on pages 172 to 177.

13 Arrange and secure the bottom tier on the left-hand side of the cake drum, leaving a 3cm (1^1/$_8$") margin on the left.

Tutor Tip

Assemble the cake-top decoration so that the centre of the top cake is placed at the centre of the cake drum.

Secure the two large blue sugarpaste baubles with royal icing, one behind the other on the right-hand side of the cake. Place the middle tier so that it sits towards the right-hand side of the bottom tier and secure.

14 Secure the bauble Christmas tree onto the top tier with royal icing. Place and secure the Christmas tree and top tier towards the left of the middle tier. With royal icing, secure the 3cm–8cm (1^1/$_8$"–3^1/$_8$") decorated baubles in the arrangement of your choice on the cake and board.

Baubles and Christmas Tree

Edibles

500g (1lb ¾oz) sugarpaste: white (SK)

200g (7oz) SK Instant Mix Royal Icing

100g (3½oz) SK Sugar Florist Paste (SFP): Pale Blue, White

SK Professional Paste Food Colours: Bluebell, Mint, Rose, Violet

SK Professional Liquid Food Colours: Bluebell, Mint

SK Designer Metallic Lustre Dust Food Colour: Light Gold

SK Designer Moon Beam Dust Food Colour: Jade

SK Designer Bridal Satin Lustre Dust Food Colour: Damask Rose, Delphinium, Lavender, Myrtle, White Satin

SK Gold Ball Dragées: 3mm (¹/₈")

SK Gold and Silver Flake

SK Sugar Sprinkles: Blue

Gelatine (SK)

SK Edible Glue

Clear alcohol

Equipment

Round polystyrene balls: seven x 2cm (¾"), five x 2.5cm (1"), thirteen x 3cm (1¹/₈"), six x 4cm (1½"), one x 5cm (2"), one x 6cm (2³/₈"), one x 7cm (2¾"), three x 8cm (3¹/₈")

12.5cm (5") round cake board

Round cutter: 2cm (¾")

3mm (¹/₈") strip cutter (JEM)

Embosser of your choice

1.5cm (½") daisy cutter (PME)

Textured rolling pin of your choice

Piping nozzles: nos. 0, 1, 3, 101s

How to cover the baubles

1 Colour the sugarpaste and SFP with the respective food colours so that the pastes are ready to use.

2 Roll out the sugarpaste to approximately 3mm (¹/₈") thick and cut out circles that are about twice the size of the polystyrene balls. Lightly cover the balls with edible glue and cover with sugarpaste in the colours described below, or your own choice of colours. Dart in four places around the base to fit the paste around the ball shape, trim off the excess paste and roll the balls in both hands to smooth the surface.

Decoration

3 Large blue baubles: Cover the 8cm (3¹/₈") baubles with pale blue sugarpaste. When the sugarpaste covering starts to dry, tie together both ends of a piece of

cotton thread to make a loop. Insert a dress pin at the top of a ball and put the loop around it. Stretch the thread around the bottom of the ball and bring it back up to the dress pin from the opposite side. Repeat the same process moving 90° around the ball to make four lines. Repeat until you get the desired number of dividing lines and then roll the ball with both hands to make the surface smooth. Remove the thread once the sugarpaste is dry. Add piped flower patterns following the instructions for decorating the sides of the top tier (see page 169).

4 Green baubles: Lightly mix white and green sugarpaste, roll out and cover each ball as before. Roll out some Green SFP, make a band of about 3mm (under ¾") wide with a strip cutter and glue it around the middle of a ball. Indent either side of the band with a ball tool and glue gold dragées to it.

5 Blue baubles: Lightly mix white and blue sugarpaste, then roll out and cover each ball. Press the embosser of your choice onto the surface to inscribe patterns. Use a no. 0 nozzle to pipe white

royal icing over the patterns marked in the paste. When dry, mix White Satin dust food colour with clear alcohol and paint over the iced pattern with a fine paintbrush.

6 Pale green baubles: Cover each ball with pale green sugarpaste. Thinly roll out some White SFP, cut out several flowers with a daisy cutter and glue them around the ball. Make an indent at the centre of each flower with a small ball tool.

7 Dissolve some gelatine in the same amount of hot, boiled water and colour

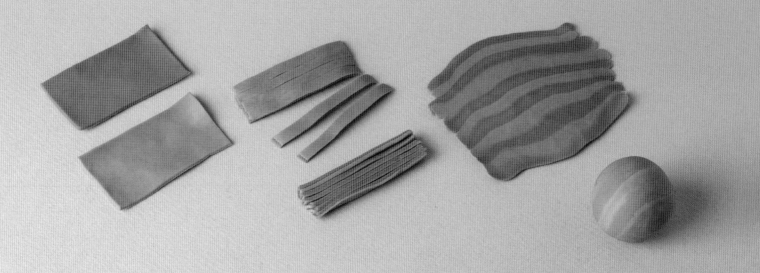

with Mint liquid food colour. Before the gelatine mixture cools, place it into a piping bag and snip off the very end of the bag so you have a very small hole to pipe through. Pipe dots onto greaseproof paper with a piping bag. Leave the dots to dry, then glue them to the centre of each of the flowers.

8 Pink and purple baubles: Roll out the pink and purple sugarpaste to 2mm (under ¼") thick and cut them into rectangles of the same size. Place two rectangles on top of each other and cut both into strips that are 5mm (¼") wide. To make a stripy pattern, lay all the strips side-by-side with the cut edges of each strip facing upwards, as shown in the picture. Roll out the sugarpaste and repeat the steps to cover all the balls.

9 Pale blue baubles: Cover the balls with pale blue sugarpaste. Pressure pipe petals with pale blue royal icing in a piping bag fitted with a no. 1 nozzle. Press blue sugar sprinkles into the petals and the paste and glue gelatine dots (see step 7) in the centre with edible glue.

10 Pink ribbon baubles: Lightly mix the pink and purple sugarpastes, roll the paste

out and cover the balls. Roll out some pink SFP and use a textured rolling pin to mark patterns onto the paste. Cut out a strip long enough to wrap around the ball as a ribbon and glue in place.

> ### Tutor Tip
>
> Dust the decorated balls with the lustre dust colour of your choice and decorate with gold or silver flakes and dragées for an extra festive touch.

Christmas tree

11 Cover a 12.5cm (5") round cake board with blue sugarpaste (see page 35). Cover two 2cm (¾"), one 2.5cm (1") and two 3cm (1⅛") polystyrene balls with the same blue sugarpaste, as described in step 2. Roll and flatten a ball of sugarpaste and glue it to the centre of the board.

12 Push the balls onto a skewer, one on top of the other. Place the 3cm (1⅛") polystyrene balls on the skewer first, then place the 2.5cm (1") ball on next, followed finally by the 2cm (¾") balls, so that the smallest ball is on top. Press the skewer

into the ball of sugarpaste on the board so that it stands centrally on the board and allow to dry. Cut off any skewer protruding from the 2cm (¾") ball.

13 To make the bottom row of the tree, cut out five discs of pale green sugarpaste that are 2cm (¾") in diameter and glue them evenly around the skewered polysytrene balls. Arrange and secure the 4cm (1½") baubles on top.

14 To build up the tree, glue 2cm (¾") sugarpaste circles where you want to attach the baubles. Place the following sizes and numbers of baubles on each row:

2nd row: 5 x 3cm (1¼")
3rd row: 5 x 3cm (1¼")
4th row: 4 x 2.5cm (1")
5th row: 4 x 2cm (¾")
6th row: 1 x 2cm (¾")

15 Thinly roll out some Pale Blue SFP and make several 1cm (³/₈") x 20.5cm (8") strips. Dust Jade dust food colour over both sides and twist loosely. Stick these ribbons around the edges of the board, taking care to hide the joins.

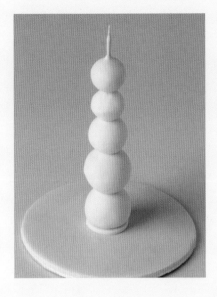

These baubles are a fun idea for the festive season. They can be used as Christmas tree decorations, festive ornaments or can be stacked to make a table centrepiece.

Christmas Couture Cake

Favour Ideas

This section includes pretty and contemporary decoration ideas for cupcakes, cookies and mini cakes that would make great accompaniments for your main wedding cake. These quick and easy favour ideas can be styled to complement the theme of your big day and would make fabulous personalised gifts for your guests.

Baking and covering cupcakes

Edibles

50g (1¾oz) cake mixture per muffin case (use your own recipe or see recipes on pages 10 to 15)

70g (2½oz) sugarpaste per cupcake (SK)

Equipment

Muffin cases

Muffin tin

Wire cooling rack

Sharp knife

1 Preheat the oven to 180°C/350°F/gas mark 4.

2 Make the cake mixture using your chosen recipe. Fill each muffin case about ²/₃ full and bake for around 20 minutes or until they bounce back to the touch.

3 Leave to cool for a few minutes and then turn out from the tin onto a wire rack.

4 Once the cakes have cooled, take them out of the muffin cases. Trim off the top of the cupcake to make it level and spread a thin layer of buttercream, ganache or jam over the cake.

5 Roll out the sugarpaste to 5mm (¼") thick. Place the sugarpaste over the cupcake and smooth it down with your hands. If the sugarpaste is too wide at the base, cut darts into the side of the paste with clean scissors, then roll out and smooth the surface of the paste with both hands. Use a sharp knife to trim any excess sugarpaste from the base of the cupcake.

Tutor Tip

Only cover the mini cake with a very thin layer of buttercream, jam or ganache so that the filling doesn't soak through the sugarpaste and spoil the look of the cake.

Bride and groom cupcakes

Edibles

Cupcakes: 5cm (2") base x 7cm (2¾") top x 5cm (2") deep

30g (1oz) sugarpaste per cupcake: white (SK)

12g (½oz) modelling paste per cupcake: white (50:50 Mexican Modelling Paste (MMP) and Sugar Florist Paste (SFP))

SK Silver Ball Dragées

A small amount of royal icing (SK)

SK Edible Glue

Equipment

Basic equipment (see pages 6 to 7)

Round cutters: 4cm, 4.5cm, 5cm, 5.5cm (1½", 1¾", 2", 2¼")

Cupcake wrappers: Zebra Black and Lace Flower

Ribbons: black satin and white chiffon

Miniature diamanté crown and tiara

Bridegroom

1 Roll out the white sugarpaste to 1cm (³⁄₈") thick, cut out the paste with a 4cm (1½") round cutter and leave to dry.

2 Thinly roll out some modelling paste and cut out the paste with a 5cm (2") round cutter. Cover the sugarpaste with this modelling paste and stick down at the back with edible glue. Make dents around the edge of the paste with a ball tool and attach a silver dragée at each mark with a small amount of royal icing.

3 Cover the cupcake with white sugarpaste and wrap the cake in a zebra black cupcake wrapper. Secure the circle of paste onto the cupcake with royal icing. Make a bow out of black ribbon and attach it to the front of the cupcake wrapper with double-sided tape so that it looks like a bow tie. To finish, place a miniature crown on top of the circle of paste. Make sure the crown is removed before the cake is eaten.

Bride

1 Roll out the white sugarpaste to 5mm (¼") thick and cut out the paste with a 4.5cm (1¾") round cutter. Leave it to dry.

2 Repeat the steps for the bridegroom cupcake using silver dragées and a lace flower cupcake wrapper. Finish with a miniature tiara and attach a chiffon ribbon at the back. Make sure the tiara is removed before the cake is eaten.

Gift box mini cakes

Tutor Tip

Bake mini cakes in the same way as cupcakes but use an individual mini cake tin rather than a muffin tin. Each individual cake tin should be greased well or lined with greaseproof paper before being filled with cake mixture.

Edibles

Square sponge cakes: 5cm (2") x 5cm (2") x 5cm (2") each

60g (2oz) sugarpaste per mini cake: pale blue (SK)

A small quantity of white royal icing (SK)

5g–10g (¼oz–½oz) modelling paste: white (50:50 Mexican Modelling Paste (MMP) and Sugar Florist Paste (SFP))

SK Designer Bridal Satin Lustre Dust Food Colour: White Satin

Equipment

Basic equipment (see pages 6 to 7)

Diamanté pearl flower decoration or similar

Piping nozzle: no. 0

Piping bag

Small posy pick

1 Roll out the pale blue sugarpaste and cover the cake in the same way as for a large square cake (see page 34).

2 Thinly roll out some modelling paste and cut out two strips that are 1.2cm x 15cm (³/₈" x 6") in size and two strips that are 1.5cm x 12cm (½" x 5") in size. Dust all four strips with White Satin lustre dust.

3 Place the two 1.2cm x 15cm (³/₈" x 6") strips across the cake so that they cross over at the top and look like ribbons. Stick them down with edible glue and use a no. 0 nozzle and white royal icing to pipe dots along both sides of the ribbons.

4 Pleat the two remaining pieces of paste and place them on top of the cake to make the bow. Insert a posy pick just behind the bow and attach a diamanté pearl flower or similar decoration into the pick. Make sure the pick and decoration are safely removed before the cake is eaten.

Floral mini cakes

Edibles

Round sponge cakes: each 5cm (2") x 5cm (2") deep

60g (2oz) sugarpaste: white (SK)

5g–10g (¼oz–½oz) modelling paste: white (50:50 Mexican Modelling Paste (MMP) and Sugar Florist Paste (SFP))

10g (¼oz) SK Sugar Florist Paste (SFP): White

SK Bridal Satin Lustre Dust Food Colours: Double Cream, White Satin

A small quantity of white royal icing (SK)

Equipment

Basic equipment (see pages 6 to 7)

Strip cutter: 3mm (¹/₈")

Frill cutter

Large carnation cutter

Bead maker: 3mm (¹/₈")

Piping nozzle: no. 0

Scriber

1 Roll out the white sugarpaste and cover the cake in the same way as the cupcakes (see page 178).

2 Make vertical lines down the cake by pushing a 3mm (¹/₈") strip cutter into the paste and make a dent in the top of the cake with a ball tool. Dust the surface of the cake with a soft brush and Double Cream lustre dust.

3 Use a scriber to make marks around the cake that are 1cm (³/₈") apart and 1.5cm (½") from the bottom of the cake. Roll out the modelling paste and use a frill cutter to cut out a strip that is 2.5cm (1") wide. Cut the strip into 3cm (1¹/₈") pieces of paste and frill each of them with a cocktail stick. Attach the middle of the frilled strips to the marks at the sides of the cake with edible glue. Use a no. 0 nozzle and white royal icing to pipe dots along the middle of the frills and around the sides of the cake. When they are fully dry, dust the frills and the dots with White Satin lustre dust.

4 Thinly roll out some White SFP, cut out six petals with a carnation cutter and dust the petals with White Satin lustre dust. Frill the edge of the petals with a bone tool and fold the flower into quarters. Pinch the base of the paste to make a mini carnation and use edible glue to attach six mini carnations to the dent on top of the cake.

5 Dust a bead maker with White Satin lustre dust and use white modelling paste to make pearl beads (see instructions for how to make the lace dragonfly in the Bird of Joy cake, page 158). Glue the pearl beads around the mini carnation bouquet with edible glue.

Rose cupcakes

Edibles

Cupcakes: 7cm (2¾") x 3cm (1⅛") deep

80g (2¾oz) piping buttercream per cupcake (see page 21), coloured with Rose liquid or paste food colour

30g (1oz) piping buttercream per cupcake, coloured with Leaf Green liquid or paste food colour

30g (1oz) sugarpaste: white (SK)

SK Edible Glue

Equipment

Basic equipment (see pages 6 to 7)

Cupcake wrapper of your choice

Greaseproof paper, cut into squares

Piping nozzles: nos. 67, 104

7cm (2¾") round cutter

1 Fit a piping bag with a no. 104 nozzle and fill a ⅓ full with buttercream.

2 Use the buttercream to secure a square of greaseproof paper onto a flower nail. With the flat side of the nozzle, pipe a short line of buttercream in the centre of the paper. Hold the bag vertically and place the thick part of the nozzle in the centre of the line. Pipe a narrow cylinder by turning the nail 1½ times. Starting halfway up from the bottom of the first cylinder, pipe and overlap a second cylinder for 1½ turns.

3 Pipe a petal turning the nail anti-clockwise with your left hand. If you are left-handed, turn the nail clockwise with your right hand.

4 For the inner petals, hold the bag in the same position as before and evenly pipe three petals around the cylinder. Pipe thee petals within one rotation of the nail; the petals should be higher than the top of the second cylinder.

5 For the outer petals, turn the nozzle slightly towards the outside and pipe five petals around the inner petals. Pipe five petals within one rotation of the nail and try to overlap them. Put the roses, still attached to the paper, on a tray and leave them to chill in the refrigerator until they are firm.

6 Roll out some white sugarpaste to 3mm (⅛") thick and cut out with a 7cm (2¾") round cutter. Spread buttercream thinly over the top of the cake and place the sugarpaste over the buttercream. Use a ball tool to make seven dents in the sugarpaste: one at the centre and six around the centre. Wrap the cupcake in a wrapper of your choice.

7 Once the roses are firm, remove them from the greaseproof paper and trim away any excess buttercream underneath the rose with scissors. Put a small amount of edible glue on the central dent in the sugarpaste and use a palette knife to place a rose onto it. Secure six roses to the other dents in the sugarpaste in the same way as the first one.

8 Fit a piping bag with a no. 67 nozzle and ½-fill with green buttercream. Hold the bag at an angle of 45° and place the nozzle horizontally across the base of the rose. Pressure pipe at first then relax the pressure gradually, lifting the bag to 45° and pulling away to stop. Neaten the tip of the leaf with your fingers. Pipe leaves at the base of the roses around the cupcake.

Tutor Tip

You can also make these roses with firm-peak royal icing following the same process, but you should leave them to dry at room temperature rather than in the refrigerator.

Wedding dress cookies

Edibles

Dress-shaped cookies (see recipe on page 16)

SK Instant Mix Royal Icing and Run-Out Icing: white

SK Sugar Florist Paste (SFP): Pale Green, White

SK Designer Bridal Satin Lustre Dust Food Colour: White Satin

Equipment

Paper and acetate piping bags
Piping nozzle: no. 0

See page 28 for tips on working with run-out icing.

1 Fill an acetate piping bag with white royal icing and snip the tip off the piping bag to about the size of a no. 0 or no. 1 nozzle. Pipe around the outline of the cookie.

2 Fill another piping bag with run-out icing then snip slightly more from the end so the tip is slightly larger than the one used for the outline. Flood inside the outline with white run-out icing and leave to dry.

3 Once dry, decorate the bust and hem of the dress with small loops of white royal icing, piping continuously with a no.

0 nozzle (known as filigree or the Cornelli technique). Once dry, dust White Satin lustre dust over the dress.

4 Roll out some White SFP and cut out a 1.5cm (½") circle, six 4cm (1½") ovals and two 2cm x 7cm (¾" x 2¾") strips. Fold the ovals in half, wrap them to make roses and dust them with White Satin dust to finish.

5 Cut one end of each strip diagonally and gather the opposite end. Use royal icing to pipe small loops onto the diagonal ends of the paste in the same style as the dress. Attach the circle of paste to the waist of the dress with a small amount of royal icing.

6 Make some small leaves and stems with Pale Green SFP and attach them to

the circle of paste, then add the roses with edible glue. Attach the gathered sides of the strips to the back of the dress with a small amount of royal icing.

Tutor Tips

You can make several different types of dress from two different long dress cookie cutters – one with a wide skirt and another with a fitted skirt. Create your own style of dress by changing the length of the skirt and the neckline before you bake them.

Use different cutters and colours to make dresses and accessories for the bridesmaids, flower girls and even the guests.

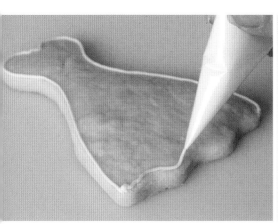
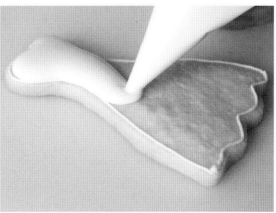

Guide to Making Sugar Flowers

Cutting out petals with cutters/templates

1 Lightly grease a non-stick board with white vegetable fat and thinly roll out some SFP with a non-stick rolling pin or a CelStick.

2 Cut out the petals with a flower cutter or a cutting wheel with a template. For a neat cut, lightly grease the cutter with white vegetable fat.

Tutor Tip

Make sure to keep any SFP you are not working with sealed in a food-grade plastic bag so that it does not dry out.

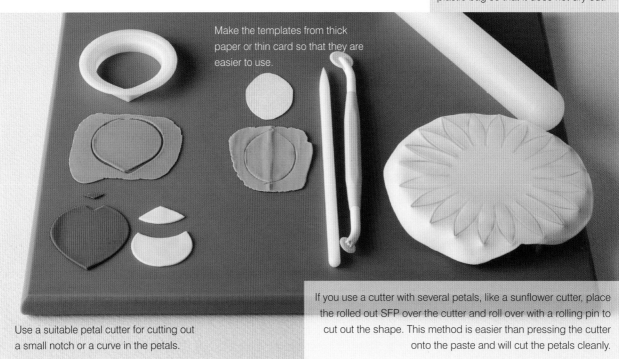

Make the templates from thick paper or thin card so that they are easier to use.

Use a suitable petal cutter for cutting out a small notch or a curve in the petals.

If you use a cutter with several petals, like a sunflower cutter, place the rolled out SFP over the cutter and roll over with a rolling pin to cut out the shape. This method is easier than pressing the cutter onto the paste and will cut the petals cleanly.

Making wired petals and leaves

Tutor Tips

Make sure you cover each floral wire with edible glue before you insert it into a petal or leaf to hold it firmly in place.

Insert the wire all the way up to the very end of the petal or leaf. The wire will allow you to curve the flower with your fingers and will make it stronger.

Small wired petals and leaves

The most efficient way to make several small petals and leaves at the same time is to roll out a long strip of paste, leaving a mound for the wire in each petal/leaf. Using the mounds as a guide, you can cut out several petals or leaves from the paste.

1 Roll out a long strip of SFP, leaving a mound of paste in the centre for a wire.

2 Gently insert a glued floral wire into the mound of the petal or leaf. With your fingers, hold either side of the mound to prevent the wire from sticking out of the paste.

Small wired petals and leaves   Long wired petals and leaves

Large wired petals and leaves   Flower base (polystyrene)

Veining petals and leaves

Specially-designed veiners

Large wired petals and leaves

The most efficient way to make large wired petals and leaves is to lay one thin piece of SFP on top of another and place the wire in between the layers of paste.

1 Thinly roll out some SFP and cut into two pieces. Line up some glued wires on one piece of paste and lay the second piece of paste on top. Make sure you leave room between the wires so that you have enough paste on either side to cut out the petal or leaf.

2 Cut the paste into strips, so that each strip of paste has a wire in the centre. Use a CelStick to thinly roll out the paste around the wire and use a petal cutter or a template to cut out the petals or leaves.

Long wired petals and leaves

1 Make a sausage of SFP and insert a glued wire into it.

2 Place the wired sausage on a non-stick board. Use your fingers to roll and stretch out the sausage of paste around the wire to the length required.

3 Use a CelStick to thinly roll out the sausage of paste and cut out the shape required.

Flower base (polystyrene)

1 Use a bamboo skewer to make a hole in the polystyrene flower base and dab a small amount of edible glue in the hole.

2 Plug the hole with a small piece of SFP.

3 Make a small hook in the end of a wire and brush with edible glue. Insert the wire into the SFP and leave it to dry.

Veining petals and leaves

To emboss veins on petals, I would recommend that you use a bamboo skewer or a silk veining tool on a non-stick board. It is best to use a bamboo skewer for rectangular petals, such as the Eustoma, ginger, dahlia or daffodil and a silk veining tool for rounded petals, such as the rose, buttercups or Phalaenopsis orchid.

Roll the skewer along the paste little by little, keeping the tip of the skewer pointing towards the base of the petal.

It is best to use specially-designed veiners for leaves with more complex veins such as rose, camellia and hydrangea leaves. However, for simpler leaves place the leaf on a sponge pad and draw the lines on with a leaf-shaping tool. Make sure that the tip of the leaf shaping tool is held at an angle against the paste, otherwise you may cut through the paste.

Shaping petals and leaves

A bone tool is useful if you want to frill the edge of a petal, whereas a flower-shaping tool would be used for making gentle curves. To soften the edges of petals and leaves, roll the tool of your choice over the very edge of the paste, so that the tool is half on the paste and half on the sponge pad.

Curled edges

To curl the edges of a petal, place the petal on a sponge pad and wrap the edges around a bamboo skewer. To curl the petals of a multi-petal flower shape such as a daisy or a calyx, use a bone tool to stretch each petal outwards towards the tip, then back inwards towards the centre.

Cupping

There are three methods of cupping petals, depending on what you are making:

• Push and cup around the centre of a petal with a ball tool on a sponge pad in a circular motion.

• Push the centre of a floweret with a small ball tool on a sponge pad.

• Place a petal over a ball of polystyrene and make a cup to fit the curve by pinching any excess paste at the centre of the base.

Tutor Tip

To make your flowers look as natural as possible, it is important to smooth out and thin the very edges of each leaf or petal, even if the leaves and petals are supposed to be quite thick.

Mexican hat technique

The Mexican hat technique is useful for making the basic shape of small, deep flowers such as the daffodil.

1 Press a circle of SFP against the hole of a sponge pad to make a cone in centre.

2 Remove the paste from the foam pad and place onto a non-stick board, with the cone facing upwards. Use a CelStick to roll out the paste around the cone, then put the appropriate cutter over the cone and cut out the shape.

3 Stretch the ends of the petals with a bone tool on the sponge pad from the underside to make them curl outward.

4 Place the rounded end of a CelStick in the centre of the flower and gather the petals around the stick.

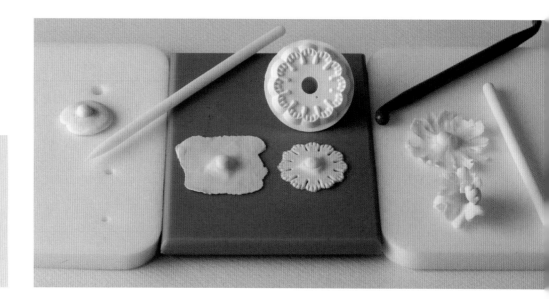

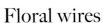

Colouring petals and leaves

Dust colours are most commonly used to achieve natural shading on flowers. Mix your chosen dust food colours in a palette, blot any excess colour onto kitchen paper and dust over the petals or leaves with a soft brush. Make sure to dust the petals or leaves before the paste dries out, as this will ensure that the colours stay vivid. If you use are using darker dust food colours then it is a good idea to pass the dusted petals or leaves through the steam of a kettle to set the colour. However, you should only do this two or three times for each petal or leaf as too much steam can make the dust colours look unnatural.

Alternatively, you can mix dust or paste food colours with a drop of clear alcohol and paint the petals or leaves with a fine paintbrush. I have used this technique for the camellia and spider plant in this book.

In order to give your leaves a shiny finish paint confectioners' glaze over their surface with a paintbrush. Clean your paintbrushes afterwards with confectioners' glaze cleaner which is available from sugarcraft suppliers.

Floral wires

The higher the gauge number, the finer the wire. The gauge required depends on the size of the petal or leaf you want to make. Hold the wires straight when you cut them with wire cutters or pliers.

Commonly used wires

32-gauge wire for vines: coil a 32-gauge wire around a bamboo skewer or the handle of a paintbrush curl it.

30-gauge white wire (for petals)

30-gauge green wire (for leaves)

28- to 20-gauge hooked wires for flower centres or bases: hook the end of the wire with pliers so that it does not fall out of the base.

20-gauge wire for U-shaped pins: cut a wire to 5cm–6cm (2"–2¼") long and bend into a 'U' shape with pliers. U-shaped pins are useful for fixing bouquets neatly to a cake.

Keeping the shape of petals and leaves

It is important to support your flowers whilst they dry so that they retain their shape. Tissues and thin aluminum foil are both flexible and ideal for keeping safe any size or shape of sugar flower.

Flower stand

Flower stands are specifically made to support wired sugar flowers whilst they are drying. Use the holes to hang wired petals and small flowers until they hold their shape.

Aluminium foil

Cut a square of aluminium foil, make a cut from the edge to the centre of the foil and wrap the foil around the flower to prevent the petals from opening.

Tissue paper/kitchen paper

Tear a piece of tissue paper into strips and fold each piece round to make a ring. Place a petal inside the ring so that the tissue paper is supporting it in a gentle cupped shape and leave to dry.

Polystyrene block

If you are using a thick wire (more than 24-gauge), push the end into a block of polystyrene once the flower centre is dry enough to hold its shape.

Taping sugar flowers and attaching sprays

Use floral tape cut to half-width to tape a wire or a small bunch of flowers together and full-width tape for a larger bunch.

Taping single stems

1 Stretch the tape to release the glue.

2 Place the tape around a wire, just below the flower head or the base of the leaf.

3 Holding the wire in one hand, squeeze the tape and the wire with your fingers with the other hand. Twist it firmly so the tape sticks to the wire.

4 Once the tape is attached, continue to tape down the wire, pulling the tape as taut as possible.

Binding a spray

Add the taped stems or the bunches one by one when you bind them into a bouquet by taping them together.

1 Tape each individual wire with green half-width floral tape.

2 Tape a small leaf to a bud and then add another leaf to the bud by taping with half-width tape.

3 Tape two flowers and add one or two large leaves using full-width tape.

4 Set the flower bunch at the centre of the spray. Add the bud bunch and the leaves to the flower bunch by taping them closely to make a compact spray.

Securing a spray to a cake with a posy pick

Fill a posy pick with a small amount of sugarpaste, then insert the pick into the top of the cake where you want your spray to sit. Pinch together the stems of the spray with a U-shaped pin and secure the bouquet into the pick. Large leaves are good for hiding a posy pick, if necessary.

To secure a large spray on the cake, as seen in the Camellia, English Rose and Tropical cakes, use 2–3 posy picks filled with sugarpaste and secure them with 2–3 U-shaped pins.

Tutor Tip

You can always use a dummy cake for any tier with a large spray. This makes the cake lighter and avoids damaging the real cake. You can arrange the spray on the dummy well in advance.

Securing a bouquet with sugarpaste

Make a ball of sugarpaste and secure it to the cake or board with edible glue. Push the wires from the flowers into the sugarpaste. You can usually fix a small spray or a large flower onto the cake using this method, which is useful for attaching flowers where you cannot insert a posy pick.

IMPORTANT NOTE

Never push wires directly into a cake or covering that is to be eaten and always remove any wired flowers, posy picks and other inedible items safely before the cake is cut.

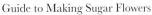

Flower Index

Templates

Camellia Cake

pages 42 to 51

Camellia Cookies, pages 50 to 51

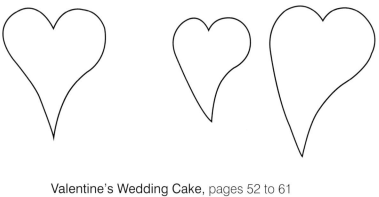

Valentine's Wedding Cake, pages 52 to 61

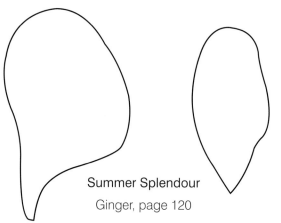

Summer Splendour

Ginger, page 120

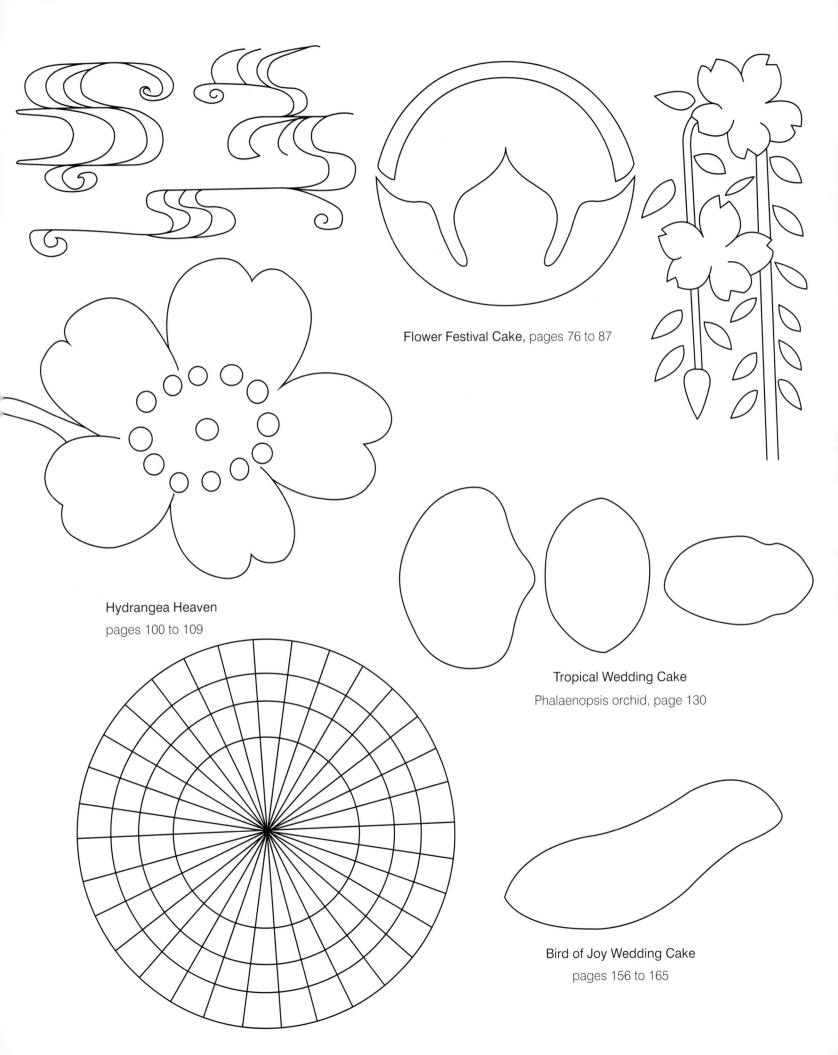

Flower Festival Cake, pages 76 to 87

Hydrangea Heaven

pages 100 to 109

Tropical Wedding Cake

Phalaenopsis orchid, page 130

Bird of Joy Wedding Cake

pages 156 to 165

Suppliers

Squires Kitchen, UK

3 Waverley Lane
Farnham
Surrey
GU9 8BB
0845 61 71 810
+44 1252 260 260
www.squires-shop.com

Squires Kitchen International School

The Grange
Hones Yard
Farnham
Surrey
GU9 8BB
0845 61 71 812
+44 1252 260262
www.squires-school.co.uk

Squires Kitchen, France

+33 (0) 1 82 88 01 66
clientele@squires-shop.fr
www.squires-shop.fr

Squires Kitchen, Italy

www.squires-shop.it

Squires Kitchen, Spain

+34 93 180 7382
cliente@squires-shop.es
www.squires-shop.es

Stockists

UK

A Piece of Cake
Thame
www.sugaricing.com

Jane Asher Party Cakes
London
020 7584 6177

Surbiton Art & Sugarcraft
Surrey
020 8391 4664

Japan

Kitchen Master
Tokyo, Japan
+81 (0) 422 41 2251
www.kitchenmaster.jp

Okashino-mori
Tokyo, Japan
+81 (3) 3841 9009
www.okashinomori.com

Witchcraft Corporation
Tokyo, Japan
+81 (3) 5430 8350
www.witchs.net

Taiwan

Holly Ocean International Ltd.
New Taipei City, Taiwan
+886 (2) 8522 8337
www.baking104.com.tw

SK Distributors

UK

Guy Paul & Co. Ltd.
Buckinghamshire
www.guypaul.co.uk

Culpitt Ltd.
Northumberland
www.culpitt.com

Australia & New Zealand

Zoratto Enterprises
New South Wales
+61 (2) 9457 0009

Sweden

Tårtdecor
Kungälv
www.tartdecor.se

Manufacturers

Smeg UK Ltd.
www.smeguk.com
www.smeg50style.co.uk

Italian appliance manufacturer
Smeg produces distinctive domestic
appliances combining design,
performance and quality.

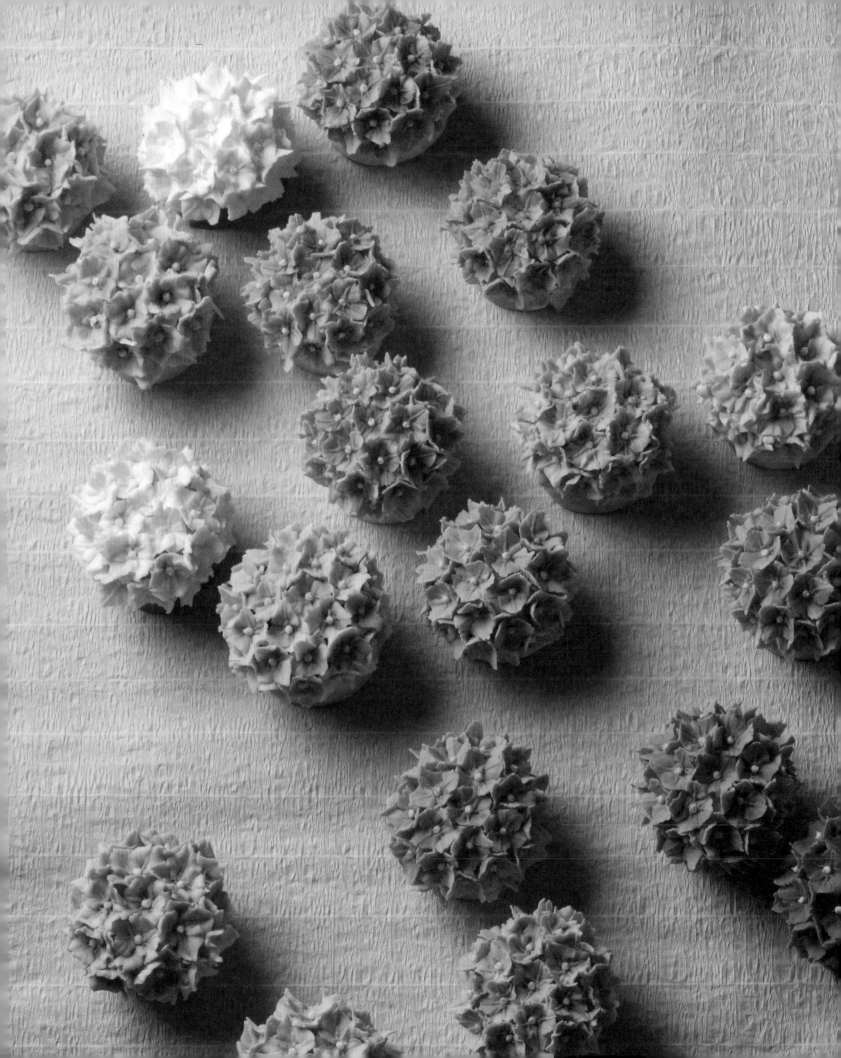